MICROS AND ART:

Lesson Plans, a Directory of Software for Achieving Educational Objectives and Procedures for Evaluating Software

Debra A. Davis
Fritz J. Erickson
and
John A. Vonk

Part C contributed by
John B. Cooney

University of Northern Colorado

 Learning Publications, Inc.
Holmes Beach, Florida

D1451349

Library of Congress Number: 86-80554

Learning Publications, Inc.
P.O. Box 1326
Holmes Beach, Florida 33509

Cover Design by Karen LeMonte

Paperback: ISBN   0-918452-90-2

Printing: 1 2 3 4 5 6 7 8   Year: 6 7 8 9

Printed and bound in the United States of America

Preface

While the Micros and Art software directory includes a near complete listing of commercially available software for teaching art concepts, it is impossible to identify every piece of software. In future additions we will continue to add titles. If you are aware of any software that should be included in this directory, please send us your suggestions; preferably in the format used in the directory. Please mail your suggestions to:

Micros and Art
Learning Publications
P.O. Box 1326
Holmes Beach, FL 33509

We have also made a serious attempt to verify the validity and accuracy of each software listing, it's appropriate concept and it's hardware requirements. Of course, prices of software are subject to change and revision. We suggest that you check with the manufacturer or your distributor for current prices and availability. In addition, we make no representation or warranty regarding the contents hereof and specifically disclaim any implied warranties or merchantability or fitness for any particular purpose of any software or equipment. We also reserve the right to revise this publication and make periodic changes in the content hereof without obligation to notify any person or organization of such revision or changes.

Following is a list of names used throughout this book which are registered trademarks of the indicated companies.

Apple Computer Company:	Apple II, Apple II+, Apple IIE, Apple IIC, MacIntosh
Atari, Inc.:	Atari 400, Atari 600, Atari 800, Atari 1200, Atari 600XL, Atari 800XL and Atari 1200XL
Commodore Business Machines:	Commodore 64
International Business Machines:	IBM PC, IBM PC JR, IBM PC XT, IBM PC AT
Tandy Corporation:	Radio Shack TRS-80 Models I-IV, Model 16

ACKNOWLEDGEMENTS

We would like to express our deepest gratitude to John B. Cooney for his valuable contribution to this project. John's insights into human information processing theory served as a catalyst for many sections of this project. We also acknowledge the editorial contributions of Learning Publications, Inc. Their staff served to provide significant help in the development of this book.

Table of Contents

Introduction vii

Part A   Lesson Plans 1

    1. Design Elements: Line, Shape and Texture 3
    2. Design Elements: Line 5
    3. Shape and Volume 9
    4. Texture 13
    5. Color 17
    6. Space - Positive and Negative 19
    7. Design Principles: Pattern and Repetition 21
    8. Balance - Symmetrical and Assymetrical 23
    9. Harmony - Rhythm 27
   10. Variety - Contrast and Elaboration 31
   11. Movement 33
   12. Illustration 35
   13. Artistic Methods - Perspective 37
   14. Artistic Methods - Animation 41
   15. Interior Design 43
   16. Artistic Methods - Commercial Design 45

Part B   Software Directory 47

    1. Animation 49
    2. Draw and Paint 55
    3. Graphic Utility 79
    4. Picture and Shapes 87
    5. Three Dimensional Graphics 93
    6. Tutorial 95

Part C   Evaluating Software for Learning Outcomes 97

Appendices

    A. Software Titles - Index 115
    B. Publishers Listing - Index 121
    C. Sample Software Evaluation Form 127

Introduction

Micros and Art is organized around three major themes. The first theme is integrating microcomputer applications into art through model lesson plans based on learning outcomes. Second, is a directory of currently available software for the art teacher. And third, procedures for evaluating software.

Lesson plans provide for integrating into art instruction activities involving computer use. These lesson plans may be modified to meet individual teaching styles. Further, each lesson may be modified to be used with one computer or with several computers in a computer lab. For this reason lessons are not sequential. Each lesson plan includes a set of computer activities plus off computer activities that may be used to reinforce desired skills and knowledge. Many topics can easily be adapted to full quarter or semester topics as well as daily or weekly lessons.

The software directory provides a list of available art software. However, this software directory is not intended to be an endorsement of any particular software. The software directory is generally organized around the same topics as the lesson plans. Included in the software directory are: the concept to be taught, the appropriate grade levels for the software, software title and publisher, suggested retail cost, the type of computer hardware necessary to run the software and where to locate software evaluations.

The probability of educational gains in each subject area should be the focus of software evaluations. Unfortunately, most educational software evaluations are preoccupied with computer related, presentational and often superficial features of the software. For example, an evaluator may focuses on the appearance of graphics. Yet, teachers know that graphics, although they have eye appeal, may contribute little or nothing to desired student learning. Positive educational outcomes brought about by using the educational software is what is important. Using the evaluation criteria outlined in this book, teachers may increase the probability that any software they select will be appropriate for their teaching objectives.

PART A
LESSON PLANS

LESSON 1

Design Elements

Line, Shape and Texture

GRADE LEVEL: Grades 8 to 12

OBJECTIVE: Students will create a two-dimensional design using three different linear qualities.

Students will use each line to define shape and create texture in the composition.

SUGGESTED INSTRUCTIONAL TIME: Three to four 45 minute sessions

IMPORTANT TERMS: Line, Pattern, Shape, Repetition and Texture

BACKGROUND: Lines can be used to create shapes and produce patterns. Patterns of lines can also be used to stimulate the sensation of touch. When a linear pattern creates a sensation of touch, it is called implied texture.

Students will not only be learning several elements of design, they will also be experiencing some of the benefits of working on a computer. Students should be limited to three colors to keep the design from becoming too busy because of the textural interpretation of colors when using a dot matrix printer.

TEACHING SUGGESTIONS: Introduce concepts of line, shape and texture. Provide students with examples of each term independently. Once students understand line, shape and texture, explain how each concept can work together to form new compositions.

Have students create a layout on paper using cut-out rectangles and squares. Students should re-arrange these until they create a visually interesting layout. Remember, students should be limited to three colors to keep the design from becoming too busy because of the textural interpretation of colors when using a dot matrix printer. Students should trace their lay-out on the paper. This will serve as a guide.

Once students have created a shape guide, have students begin work on a computer. Choose a program which is capable of creating shapes, saving shapes and re-positioning shapes at different locations. Some examples of these types of programs are; "Complete Graphics System" and "Doodle". If the program you choose can reduce, flip or rotate the shapes they create, students will have more control and variations for creating their projects.

A word of caution: Too many manipulative factors may cause problems for the younger students. Judge the capabilities of your students and plan accordingly.

After students have completed a composition, have students save their composition on a disk. If a printer is available, have students print their compositions. This hard copy can be used in other lessons.

SUGGESTED CLASSROOM ACTIVITIES:

Provide students with computer time on a regular basis. Students should work on a variety of directed compositions. Again, monitor the students progress. Too much time spent on experimentation may lead to time problems with both the students project and computer use.

REINFORCEMENT ACTIVITIES:

If students have printouts of their computer generated compositions, make a black thermal transparency of each design. Have students cut out various color backgrounds for their designs. Try solids, areas of color and a variety of colors. Mount several arrangements on tagboard. Mat the transparencies using various backgrounds. Discuss the designs with the class. Which work well? Why? Point out that a variety of techniques can be used to add color to computer printouts. How do the backgrounds vary from the computer screen display? Do the lines define shape? Do they create texture?

4

LESSON 2

Design Elements

Line

GRADE LEVEL:	Grades 4 to 6
OBJECTIVE:	Using a draw/paint program with brush and color choices, students will design a pattern of lines. This design will contain decorative lines, with no evidence of space. That is, lines will lie on the surface, not project forward or backward into space. Students will develop an understanding of how draw and paint programs can be used to create color designs.
SUGGESTED INSTRUCTIONAL TIME:	Two to three 35 minute sessions
IMPORTANT TERMS:	Line, Decorative Pattern, Repeat and Surface
BACKGROUND:	Lines are often used to decorate many surfaces. For example, wallpaper, wrapping paper and fabrics often use lines for decoration. However, decorative lines are usually not used to create perspective. That is, decorative lines do not present the illusion of moving forward or backward in space. When used in a decorative pattern, lines do not create a sense of depth.

This lesson works well as an introduction to a draw and paint program's functions. Students will gain a better understanding of visual effects caused by various brush and color selections as they work through this lesson.

TEACHING SUGGESTIONS: Begin with a discussion of line. Ask students where they see lines in the classroom. Make a list of student responses on the chalkboard. After completing a list of objects that contain line, choose one example of decorative line and one

contain line, choose one example of decorative line and one example in which line creates a sense of depth. Discuss with students the difference between the two examples. If necessary, prompt students through a series of questions. For example, what is the difference between the chair legs and the lines created by the tiles in the floor? Depending on where you sit, will the legs of a chair be in front of each other or behind each other, creating a sense of depth. Explain spatial depth as lines appearing to be (drawn perspective) or that actually are in front of or behind each other. Use a chair to demonstrate this idea. Discuss the lines created by tiles on the floor or ceiling. Why are these lines different than the chair legs? Tiles are flat on a surface and are repeated.

Reinforce the idea that when lines are used over and over on a surface, they create a decorative pattern known as a repeat. Pick several other items listed on the chalkboard and have students explain why each item listed is an example of decorative or spatial lines.

SUGGESTED CLASSROOM ACTIVITIES:

Creating a book cover with a decorative line pattern can provide students with concrete experience in line pattern. A computer can allow students to do a great deal of experimentation. Students should be given ample opportunity to experiment. However, make sure students use lines as a decorative pattern. Begin by demonstrating a draw and paint program on a computer. Have students work along with you as you demonstrate the draw and paint program. Be sure to work through choosing a brush, various lines and colors. Once students have gone through each function, allow students adequate time to become proficient.

Instruct students to develop a pattern for the design of a book cover. Tell students that the design should not contain spatial qualities. With a draw and paint program, have students experiment and come up with a line design of their own. Once students have a design they wish to keep, direct students on how to save this image. Saved images can be printed with the use of a graphics print utility. If possible, choose a graphics print utility which allows the design to be enlarged and reversed. Reversing allows the black to be printed white and the white to be printed as black.

These designs to be used as book covers will be printed and enlarged on a photocopier. Limit students to 3 or 4 colors, to create a more definitive patterned repeat.

REINFORCEMENT ACTIVITIES:

Take the hardcopy of each student's design and make several photocopies to be joined together to make a book cover. If desired, these copies can be enlarged on a photocopier. Students may color their designs with either markers or colored pencils. Be sure to have students use the 3 or 4 colors used on the computer.

Students can use their cover designs to cover a chosen book. These books can be ones that students have written themselves. Also, the cover design can be bound around several blank pages for students to use in any writing activity such as a classroom journal. It is always a good idea to integrate art into other subjects.

LESSON 3

Shape and Volume

GRADE LEVEL: Grades 9 to 12

OBJECTIVE: Using a computer, students will manipulate a design they have previously created. Previous work should be a geometric, two dimensional design using flat color to define shapes.

SUGGESTED INSTRUCTIONAL TIME: Five to seven 50 minute sessions

IMPORTANT TERMS: Volume, Shading and Value change to defining mass

BACKGROUND: Shape is defined as a two-dimensional object, having height and width. For example, a simple square. Three-dimensional shapes, that is, volumes or masses, are created when a third dimension, depth, is added. For example, a square becomes a cube or a circle becomes a sphere when a third dimension is added.

Each side of a three-dimensional shape is called a plane. Each plane is two-dimensional, or flat.

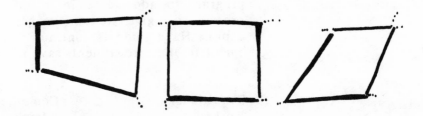

When used in combination with other planes in varying directions, planes form a three-dimensional shape. Combining planes in varying directions gives the illusion of mass or volume.

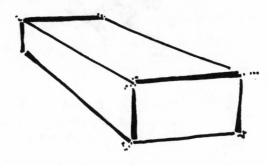

Values, varying shades of light or dark or color, can also create a sense of depth and define dimensionality. Shading and gradual value change also give a three-dimensional shape an illusion of mass or volume and depth.

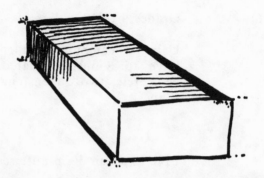

TEACHING SUGGESTIONS:

Reinforce the concepts of shape, volume, mass and value independently. Once you are sure students understand these concepts independently, make certain students understand how these concepts relate to one another. Outline the project, its objectives and process. Demonstrate computer features that students will be using to create a three-dimensional design. Let students experiment. Check to see that students are progressing as expected. Student designs should be developed from a two-dimensional design, but should now take on a three-dimensional quality by using planes, color, and value shading to create mass and volume. If an airbrush utility is available, allow students to incorporate the airbrush brush control of a computer program to add value in a more gradual manner. This process will give student images an even greater sense of depth. Have students continue working until their design is complete. Be sure students save their designs on a disk.

Traditional   Computer Manipulated
Work   Image

Using a program with geometric shape selections and freehand drawing features, students can re-work a previous design, using planes and value, or color changes, to define volume.   Triangles will become pyramids, squares will become cubes, and circles will become spheres.   Notice sections of the previous design may be eliminated to simplify the three-dimensional image.

SUGGESTED CLASSROOM ACTIVITIES:

Have students complete a two-dimensional design using a traditional technique.   Once students have created a two-dimensional design using a traditional technique, the advantages and limitations of computer graphics will be more understandable.   Be sure students have knowledge of two-dimensional shape before progressing.   Using a graphics program, allow students to manipulate their original two-dimensional design into a three-dimensional design using such variables as line, shape, placement and color choice. For example, "The Complete Graphics System," can be used for this process.   The computer will be quicker and capable of more immediate manipulation in a shorter period of time.

Be sure students save the image in various stages throughout their work.   By saving in various stages, students can experiment and still retain a beginning image, if the experimentation does not turn out to be what a student wants.

REINFORCEMENT ACTIVITIES:

Two programs which have features to, first, create three-dimensional wire images and, then, to rotate and scale the images in space, are "A2 - 3D Graphics" and "The Complete Graphics System."   Students might enjoy working with and exploring the strengths of this software.   Images created for the manipulation project can be printed or plotted depending on the hardware available in the school. If neither output devices are available, images can be photographed directly off the computer monitor screen. Images can be mounted and displayed.   Images can also be used as a basis for a sculpture project, using wire for a strict three-dimensional line interpretation or plexiglass in various colors assembled for an additive sculpture experience.

PHOTOGRAPHING TV IMAGES
(KODAK RECOMMENDATIONS)

	Film	Filter	Focal Plane Shutter Speed	Leaf Shutter Speed
Prints	Kodacolor 2 (ASA 100)	CC 40 Red	1/8 sec @ f/2.8	1/8 sec f/2.8 1/15 sec f/2
Prints	Kodacolor (ASA 400)	no filter	1/8 sec @ f/8	1/30 sec f/4
Slides	Kodachrome* (ASA 64)	CC 40 Red	1/8 sec @ f/2.8	1/8 sec f/2.8 1/15 sec f/2
Slides	Ektachrome (ASA 64)	CC 40 Red	1/8 sec @ f/2.8	1/8 sec f/2.8 1/15 sec f/2
Slides	Ektachrome (ASA 200)	no filter	1/8 sec @ f/5.6	1/30 sec f/2.8 1/8 sec f/8

*Kodachrome (ASA 64) gives higher contrast in colors, more color saturation and warmer tones.

It is recommended that all room light be off, all daylight be curtained off, and the camera be mounted on a tri-pod. A camera release should be used to trigger the shutter.

CC 40 Red filter: Cost for a glass filter is about $20.00; cost for gel with adapter is from $3.00 to $6.00 (either are special order items).

For more information on film, filter and other materials call KODAK in Oakbrook, IL, (312) 654-5300, and ask for Technical Information.

** It is suggested you tell the photo developers to hand cut the photos since the machines will sometimes start in the middle of a frame.

LESSON 4

Texture

GRADE LEVEL: Grades 3 to 5

OBJECTIVE: Printouts of patterns, colors, text or any combination of these elements will be made using a print graphics utility and/or a draw and paint program. Students will take printouts and other textual papers, implied or actual, to create a collage of a simple still life.

SUGGESTED INSTRUCTIONAL TIME: Four to five 45 minute sessions. This suggested instructional time may be lengthened if each student is expected to create their own design or pattern.

IMPORTANT TERMS: Texture (actual or implied), Pattern, Collage, and Still-life

BACKGROUND: Texture refers to how something feels. For example, the textures rough, smooth or fuzzy, can be sensed through touch. Texture can be real (actual) or by drawing one can present the illusion of texture (implied). Implied texture can be created by repeating lines or shapes, on a small scale, over an area.

Repeating lines or shapes creates a pattern. When using a computer, colors, patterns and even letters or numbers, can create an implied texture. Color is interpreted on a dot matrix printer as a different patterns. However, these patterns lack a great sense of tactile quality.

TEACHING SUGGESTIONS: To give students a better idea of texture, students should combine these high-tech textures with actual textured papers and fabrics to create their still-life collage.

Discuss texture with students. Be sure to provide examples of actual texture and implied texture. Be sure to elaborate on pattern. That is, explain how lines or shapes repeated

13

over an area create patterns. On a computer, demonstrate creation of texture. Once students understand how a computer can create texture explain the ideas of collage and still-life.

If students do not understand still-life, set up a simple still-life with 2 or 3 objects. Show students several famous works of still-lifes. Let students see actual still-life examples such as those created by Henri Fantin-Latour and Cezanne or the abstract still-lifes of Picasso. Try to also include a collage piece.

Describe collage. Point out that collage is created by shapes cut and pasted to create a picture. Be certain students understand that any textures can be used to represent an object. It is not necessary to use the one which is the same as the object.

SUGGESTED CLASSROOM ACTIVITIES:

After an introductory discussion on each concept of texture and pattern. Set up a computer in one location so that students can see a demonstration of computer developed texture. Choose a color pattern (if the program has pattern choices) or create a pattern with text, numerals, lines or shapes. For example:

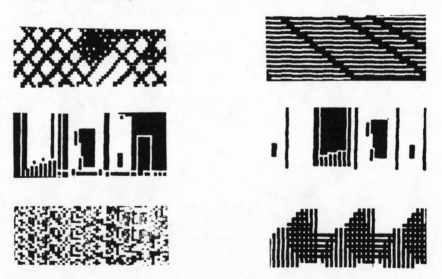

Now print out your choices so students can see how the printer interprets each feature. Continue to create textures from student suggestions. Be sure to save student choices on a disk so that these choices can be printed out at a later time (printing consumes a great deal of class time). Once the selections have been printed, make enough photocopies from which students may choose for their collage.

REINFORCEMENT ACTIVITIES:

If working in groups, let students suggest manipulations and decide on which they would like to use for their collages. This approach may be a good or schools that do not have enough work stations for individual students. With the still-life setup, instruct students to select a variety of textures, computer and actual (wallpaper, fabric scraps, wood pieces) to create their collage. Then, have students cut and paste on to construction paper or cardboard. Be sure to review the following questions. How do the high tech textures look with the actual ones? Do the high-tech textures make the picture look old-fashioned or new? Why?

LESSON 5

Color

GRADE LEVEL:

Grades 9 to 12

OBJECTIVE:

After discussing 19th century impressionistic painters, particularly Seurat, students will create a landscape composition in the Impressionistic style using a computer.

SUGGESTED
INSTRUCTIONAL
TIME:

Ten to twelve 50 minute sessions

IMPORTANT
TERMS:

Impressionism, Color Theory, Traditional Methods, Value, Hue

BACKGROUND:

Impressionism describes a style of painting used by a number of artist during the 19th century. These painters developed a painting technique to simulate the illusion of light and color reflected from objects. These 19th century painters realized the eye would mix colors which were dabbed next to each other in small amounts. For example, small dabs of red next to yellow would be interpreted as orange. This visual mixing by the eye at a distance was a new approach to color mixing. For example, dabs of yellow or red could be used with orange to create variations in hue (color) or value (light and dark). Complimentary colors could be used to dull pure color. Cool colors such as greens, blues or violets could be used to make areas recede.

If more information on color theory is needed, consult your local or school library.

TEACHING
SUGGESTIONS:

Make sure the class has a solid background in basic color theory. You may want to display a color wheel and definitions of terms in the work area for student reference. Each student should have their own workstation or this project could become over involved and time consuming.

Suggest that students sketch their landscape preliminaries on paper before beginning on the computer. Keep the composition somewhat simple, without small details. Basic contours of objects are a good idea.

17

**SUGGESTED
CLASSROOM
ACTIVITIES:**

Have students view slides or reproductions of Seurat's work. Describe the Impressionistic technique. Ask how many students have gotten extremely close to a television screen? What is the effect? Millions of small dots which form an image from a distance, similar to the Impressionistic style, are visible.

On a computer demonstrate a draw and paint program used on a computer. Demonstrate a "building-up" of a composition using an Impressionistic style. Once students understand this process, allow students to create their own Impressionistic art using a draw and paint program. Remind students that they can save their picture at any stage. Saving their picture will allow students to experiment and still save an orignal image in case the experiment needs to be done over. A program with an airbrush brush control would be extremely useful, but is not necessary for this project. Work will be quicker and will more closely simulate the Impressionistic style with this feature. "Dazzle Draw" and "Joypaint 1.1" are examples of programs with this feature. Another helpful feature is an erase option for the last manipulation used by students. This erase utility will allow immediate re-working of a mistake. Students should continue working until their projects are completed.

**REINFORCEMENT
ACTIVITIES:**

Allow students several class periods to critique their work. You may view work on a disk orby photographing the screen (See Design Elements, Lesson 3 for instructions).

Review: Was it easy to use the computer for the Impressionistic style? Discuss the limitations of the computer. Show students several examples of computer artist Saul Berstein's work as well as several by Seurat. Discuss with students the size of Seurat's "A Sunday Afternoon on the Island of La Grande Jatte" (6' 9-1/2" x 10' 1").

LESSON 6

Space – Positive and Negative

GRADE LEVEL: Grades 6 to 8

OBJECTIVE: Using the text mode of a graphics program, (e.g., "The Print Shop" or "Dazzle Draw") students will be able create a repeated pattern using various font styles and sizes of an alaphabet character.

SUGGESTED INSTRUCTIONAL TIME: Three to five 45 minute sessions for initial design. Three to five 45 minute sessions for color work.

IMPORTANT TERMS: Pattern, Repetition, Positive (figure), Negative (ground).

BACKGROUND: In a two-dimensional design, space can be positive (figure) or negative (ground). Positive space refers to the shape or object which is in/on the negative space. For example, black is usually referred to as the positive space on a negative white. Throughout this lesson, students will learn the basic concept of positive and negative by using a black series of letters on a white ground. After an initial experience with positive and negative, students will manipulate these concepts by reversing and coloring the ground and figures in a design. Letters can be changed to white on a black background while remaining the figure in a design. Only the coloring has changed, not the concept of figure/ground or positive/negative. By adding color to the figure and ground, students will further understand how these concepts are manipulated by the artist or designer.

TEACHING SUGGESTIONS: Review the concepts of pattern and repeat. Show students examples of how lettering can be used to create a two-dimensional design through repetition. Several programs which include a text mode with various type styles (fonts) also allow students to manipulate size and placement of the text. Two such programs are "Versawriter" and "Fontrix." Remember, the more versatile a program is, the more an image can be manipulated. After viewing examples of finished works, demonstrate the functions of a computer's text mode. Have one or two students try these functions as classmembers watch. Students will feel more confident if their peers can manipulate the program functions. A poster of the functions available and their results can be a helpful tool for reference during the work process. Be sure to watch students carefully for over-manipulation of their

19

designs. It is easy to get carried away with a computer graphics program. Although it is easy to over work a design, it is also easy to correct a mistake or change a color or letter position with the touch of a key or two.

SUGGESTED
CLASSROOM
ACTIVITIES:

Following an introduction, have the students begin individual designs. Begin with 10 or 15 minutes of experimentation and then move on to the actual design image. Limit students to a white screen with black lettering for the initial design. Continue until the piece is completed. Once the initial design is done, save it on a disk and have students start to re-work the design with a variety of color choices and combinations. Be sure these images are also saved on a disk.

REINFORCEMENT
ACTIVITIES:

Students may print out these designs or photograph them off the screen (see Design Elements, Lesson 3).

As a reinforcement activity, students could create an eraser print. Have students use an art gum or other soft eraser for this project. Students should begin by drawing a single letter on their eraser (the letter must be reversed to print in the proper direction, see below). Urge the students to each create a different letter in a different style.

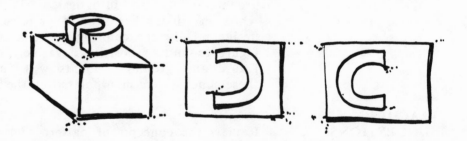

Cut around the drawn letter with an exacto knife. When the printing units are ready have the students use their letter and others to create a positive/negative design on various papers. Discuss the differences between working on computer and using the traditional printing method. What are some of the advantages of printing with the erasers? The computer designing? Which process gives the students more control? Why? Which of these approaches makes the student feel more creative?

LESSON 7

Design Principles

Pattern and Repetition

GRADE LEVEL: Grades 6 to 8

OBJECTIVE: Students will create a visual pattern using a computer text mode.

Students will demonstrate an understanding of the terms motif, pattern and repetition.

SUGGESTED INSTRUCTIONAL TIME: Six to eight 45 minute sessions

IMPORTANT TERMS: Repetition, Pattern, Motif

BACKGROUND: Pattern differs from texture in that pattern is two-dimensional, or flat, and has no tactile qualities. To create a pattern a motif must be repeated several times. For example, the letter "x" is a letter from the alphabet. However when the letter "x" is used repeatedly, it becomes a motif in a pattern. A pattern is the total of all individual motifs.

xxxxxxxxx   Each x is a motif in the total pattern.
xxxxxxxxx
xxxxxxxxx

A motif repeated in a pattern may form a visual field. In the example above, a visual field containing a rectangular shape has been created. In addition to creating patterns, motif repetition can suggest movement or create a dominant center of interest in a composition or a design.

TEACHING SUGGESTIONS: Clarify the difference between texture and pattern by using selected magazine photos. For example, a close-up photo of tree bark can represent texture. A photo of a number of trees lining a street can be used to represent a pattern. Using a variety of selected photographs, drill students on a variety of patterns and textures. Be sure students understand the difference between pattern and texture before continuing with this lesson.

Once students understand the difference between pattern and texture, explain the concept and uses of motif in pattern. Students should understand that a symbol becomes

21

motif when used repeatedly to create a pattern. On the chalkboard, draw a pattern using "x" as a motif. Have students suggest other motifs that can be used in a pattern. Explain that words can become motifs. For example:

ROO
FROOFR   cloudcl
OFROOFROOF   oudcloudcloud
ROOFROOFROOFRO   cloudcloud
HOUSEHOUSEHOUS
EHOUSEHOUSEHOU
USEHOUSEHOUSEH grassgrassgrassgrassgrass

Explain to students that each word becomes a motif in a pattern, and each pattern varies because of the motif.

SUGGESTED CLASSROOM ACTIVITIES:

On the chalkboard, develop a list of descriptive and definitive words generated through class discussion. Words such as house, roof, grass, trees and mountains are good examples. Discuss some terms that may not be appropriate such as running, walking, sleeping and swimming. From this list have students develop some simple paper and pencil outlines for their projects. Assign students to a computer and give instructions on how to access the text mode and how the text mode operates. If students are not familiar with text mode operations, you may have to provide introductory instruction.

Once students have completed a pattern and are satisfied, have students save this pattern on their disk. If a printer is available, have students print their pattern. Be sure to explain that printouts will not be in color.

Explain to students that the text mode may have a variety of type styles to choose from. Students may want to use these type styles in their patterns. In addition, students may be able to manipulate the size of their letters.

REINFORCEMENT ACTIVITIES:

Students may return to the classroom to add color to their designs using watercolors or transparent markers. Have students display their work and discuss which patterns standout more than others. Be sure to discuss the effects of adding color.

Students may wish to use a wordprocessor that is available in the school. Some primary wordprocessing instruction may be necessary. Once students feel somewhat comfortable using the word processor, have students create patterns using motifs on the word processor.

LESSON 8

Balance – Symmetrical and Assymmetrical

GRADE LEVEL: Grades 9 to 12

OBJECTIVES: Students will begin by creating two shapes to be used in their designs. These shapes may be made using free-hand drawing techniques of the computer or by combining geometric computer shapes.

Once the shapes are created, students will produce three symmetrically balanced designs and three assymetrically balanced designs.

Students will manipulate their shapes and designs by changing the positioning of the shapes, the size of the shapes, and the texture and color of the shapes or background.

SUGGESTED INSTRUCTIONAL TIME: One 50 minute session for introduction
Three to four 45 minute sessions for design development.

IMPORTANT TERMS: Balance, Symmetrical (formal), Assymmetrical (informal)

BACKGROUND: When creating artwork, balance refers to an optical equilibrium of all the parts of the picture. There are several variables which can be used to balance an artwork. Some of these variables are: position, size, color and texture. Variables such as these may be used to create symmetrical (formal) balance or asymmetrical (informal) balance. Symmetrical balance refers to an equal distribution of the parts on a vertical or horizontal axis, in a design or picture.

One unit
formally
balanced

Two units
formally
balanced

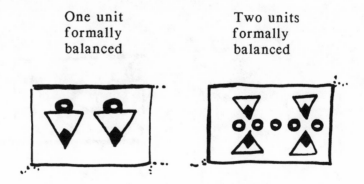

23

Symmetrical balance is usually inactive and life less because its units are repeated over and over. Formal balance is found in surface decorations such as wall paper, fabrics and wrapping papers. These items add color and interest to our environment, but they do not create a great deal of visual or emotional response.

When an artist or designer uses assymetrical balance, they create a more affective, visually striking image. Assymetrical balance can use contrasting variables to produce a visual equilibrium in an artwork.

Asymmetrical positioning of variables:

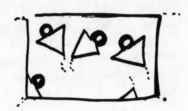

Symmetrical positioning of variables:

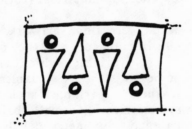

Asymmetrical balance through size variance of shapes:

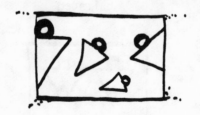

Symmetrical balance through size variance or shapes:

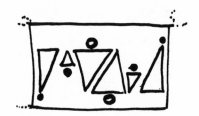

Asymmetrical color difference of balance:

Symmetrical color difference of balance:

Texture to balance: Asymmetrical   Symmetrical

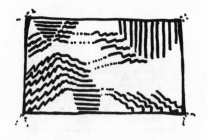 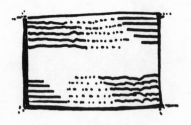

TEACHING SUGGESTIONS:

Present a thorough discussion of the two basic types of balance and the variables which students will use to manipulate their designs. Show examples of Matisse's cut paper designs and Picasso and Leger's abstract paintings. These artists used the same variables the students will be using to arrange and balance their compositions.

CLASSROOM ACTIVITIES:

On a computer demonstrate the program functions of freehand drawing, geometric shape mode, and how to add color and texture. Have the students begin their designing. Make sure they are producing three formally balanced and three informally balanced designs. Save on a disk when students are finished.

REINFORCEMENT ACTIVITIES:

Designs may be printed or photographed off the screen (see Design Elements, Lesson 3).

These designs could be printed, colored with marker and interchanged to create an abstract collage similar to Picasso's or Leger's work.

Review: Before cutting the designs for collages, discuss which are successful as asymmetrical and symmetrical examples of balance. Why do certain designs work better than others?

LESSON 9

Harmony - Rhythm

GRADE LEVEL: Grades 3 to 5

OBJECTIVE: Through a series of line manipulations this lesson will visually and interactively reinforce the concept of visual harmony created through rhythm.

This lesson will also help develop good eye-hand coordination.

**SUGGESTED
INSTRUCTIONAL
TIME:** One to two 45 minute sessions

**IMPORTANT
TERMS:** Harmony and Rhythm

BACKGROUND: Harmony is defined as a pleasing arrangement of parts in a picture or design. Harmony can be produced through a series of variables. Rhythm is one variable which can produce visual harmony. Simply stated, rhythm is a flowing repeat. In music, a flowing repeat can be referred to as meter, tempo or beat (such as a hand clap, one, two, three three three). In art, a person can create a rhythm by visually repeating a unit.

In art, each unit or shape or line can be used to create a visual rhythm in an artwork. You can show the students examples such as Jose Orzco's "Zapatistas," Giacomo Balla's "Leash in Motion," or Marcel Duchamp's "Nude Decending a Staircase". Simple rhythms can be made by repeating a line or shape. An example of a more complex rhythm can be found in a person's hair.

27

**TEACHING
SUGGESTIONS:**

To facilitate individual learning through participation, have each student at a workstation. Individual workstations helps keep students on task.

Use a program such as Koala's "Micro-Illustrator" for this project. Limit students to one color for background and one for their lines. A broad brushstroke feature will be helpful to produce a more definite representation of rhythm.

**CLASSROOM
ACTIVITIES:**

Demonstrate how the computer program you've selected for this lesson functions. Once students have been given time to learn about the software, begin the lesson. Students should follow along through a series of steps to create several examples of visual rhythm.

1. Ask students to imagine a tall standing tree. Have students imagine a strong lumberjack cutting the tree down. Students should imagine the tree beginning to fall. Students should imagine the falling tree stopping every few inches. Ask students to draw the rhythm of the tree as it falls.

2. Walk across the room, moving up and down on your toes. Have students translate this movement into a linear rhythm.

3. Have students use a diagonal line to create their next rhythm.

28

4. Show students an "S" curve of a road or the "S" formed in the neck of a flamingo. These examples may be found in magazine photographs. Ask students to produce a rhythm pattern using this type of line.

5. Select several sound effects which could be interpreted with lines. Have students draw their interpretations of different sounds. For example, sharp sounds may be represented by a zig - zag line.

Continue this lesson with other ideas for creating visual rhythm.

REINFORCEMENT ACTIVITIES:

In the classroom, have students choose one of their computer designs to re-do using construction paper. Several colors may be used. Using a computer to develop this lesson will make the difficult task, of teaching abstract concepts to the younger students, much easier. For students to create these rhythmic designs with traditional materials, much more time would be needed and students might easily lose interest.

LESSON 10

Variety – Contrast and Elaboration

GRADE LEVEL: Grades 9 to 12

OBJECTIVE: Using an image-processing (video digitizing) program, students will copy a master's artwork.

Once an image has been captured, students will re-work the image using a draw and paint program.

**SUGGESTED
INSTRUCTIONAL
TIME:**   Ten to twelve 45 minute sessions

**IMPORTANT
TERMS:**   Contrast, Elaboration, Variety and Image-processing

BACKGROUND: When all picture parts work together, these parts create harmony. Likewise, when parts are treated differently (brushstroke, texture, color or lighting) a composition exhibits variety. Variety can be created through contrasts (light and dark, smooth and rough). Elaboration is the process of reworking areas of a picture as each area interrelates to one another. Artists may add more color or smooth a line to elaborate an area of a composition. Both contrast and elaboration add to the visual interest and create variety in a total composition.

Video digitizing (image processing) is the process of capturing, computerizing and manipulating images. For more information refer to the article, "Digital Image Processors, Give Your Computer the Gift of Sight," by Owen Linzmayer, *Creative Computing*, July 1985, which further describes a digitizing process, necessary equipment and software.

**TEACHING
SUGGESTIONS:**   Using an image processor, copy an original master's work from a book or a reprint and save this work on a disk. Discuss with students the value of manipulating a master's work. Explain how students can gain an insight into the process the artist went through to create the artwork.

Each student should have their own workstation. Remind students that you are not looking for a cartoon approach to manipulating these images (e.g., no moustaches on Mona Lisa). This is a serious project. Point out to students that serious thought and execution of variety, through contrast and elaboration, is important.

31

CLASSROOM
ACTIVITIES:

Introduce the project with an explanation of the objective and examples of the desired results. Demonstrate the image processor and the steps of how it functions. Capture student images, saving them on a disk, and enter these images into a draw and paint program. Begin work on manipulation of the image. Be sure to save the work at several stages. Saving work on a disk helps prevent a good idea from being lost, by mistake.

Discuss with each student the possibilities for adding contrast and elaborating their chosen artwork. Color changes can be made to contrast the original image, or areas of the image may be erased, or reworked with textures, to elaborate on the image. Students should continue until the project is complete, and then save on a disk.

REINFORCEMENT
ACTIVITIES:

Photograph images from the computer screen (see Design Elements, Lesson 3). Enlarge these images to an 8" X 10" size, mount and display these images, with the original, if possible. Ask students to respond to the following questions: Which images worked best for this project? Was manipulation easy? What types of manipulation did each student attempt? How did each student create variety? Does the image each student reworked have greater contrast? Is the variety pleasing? Did students feel they were invading the image of the master?

LESSON 11

Movement

GRADE LEVEL: Grades 6 to 8

OBJECTIVE: Using simple shapes such as squares, circles or triangles, students will produce a static design on a computer.

Students will create an image which gives the illusion of movement.

SUGGESTED INSTRUCTIONAL TIME: Four to five 45 minute sessions

IMPORTANT TERMS: Movement, Static, Dynamic, Eye travel over the picture plane

BACKGROUND: Movement in artwork is not actual movement. That is, movement is a created illusion. The use of line, color and other design elements and principles work together to create a sense of movement in a composition. Due to the limitations of small microcomputers, this lesson will focus on two-dimensional shapes. The lesson will develop an understanding of movement of shapes on the picture plane. Shapes will not actually travel over the space. Rather, our eyes will follow the shapes.

To create a sense of movement, shapes may change in size, positioning and direction. Due to color limitations, a computer cannot properly show movement through color or value change, although both of these elements can create a sense of movement with traditional techniques.

TEACHING SUGGESTIONS: Have students sketch out several simple shape arrangements on paper before beginning to work on a computer. Be sure to explain the difference between a design which is static and lifeless, and one which shows movement and is dynamic.

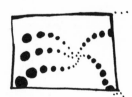 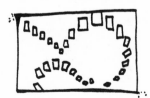 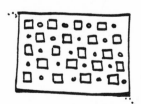

33

Access the shapes mode of a graphics program such as "Dazzle Draw," "Micro-Illustrator," "Doodle," or "Art Gallery." Demonstrate on a computer how the features of the selected program work. Be sure to add color and texture. However, be careful that color and texture do not detract from the design objective.

CLASSROOM ACTIVITIES:

Demonstrate the features of shape, color and texture. Develop an example on screen as students watch. Allow students to experiment. At individual work stations have students continue working until designs are completed. Be sure students save their finished work on a disk.

REINFORCEMENT ACTIVITIES:

Have students print out their designs. Color may be added with marker, watercolor or colored pencil. Glue each design to cardboard of various thicknesses to mount on a colored background. A dimension of depth, or relief, is added when each design is mounted to different thicknesses of cardboard, creating surface inequalities. These various thicknesses of cardboard will make movement even more evident than flat designs.

Move on to more advanced discussion of movement promted by characteristics found in a selected series of reproductions. Movement in the work of a master may not be as straight forward as the students' two-dimensional designs. Discuss why. Did the creation of the designs help students see the less obvious movement in the reproductions?

LESSON 12

Illustration

GRADE LEVEL: Grades 7 to 8

OBJECTIVE: Students will write and illustrate a short story about emotions using a computer graphics/creative writing program (e.g., "Bank Street Story Book" or "Storymaker").

Students will use an appropriate color to express emotions described in their story (e.g., sadness = blue). Symbols for such emotions may also be used to illustrate the story (e.g., loneliness = an empty room, or joy = a yellow balloon).

SUGGESTED
INSTRUCTIONAL
TIME: Eight to ten 45 minute sessions

IMPORTANT
TERMS: Symbolism, Storyline, Illustration, Prose, Color and Mood

BACKGROUND: Symbols are images which usually represent ideas or abstract feelings. For example, a heart may represent love, a medal may represent courage and an empty street may represent loneliness. In addition, certain colors may represent abstract feelings. For example, black may represent sadness, red may represent anger and blue may represent emptyness. Symbols and colors may be used to visually enhance a story when used with prose. This idea of using symbols and colors to enhance a story is the concept behind illustration. Prose refers to the words in a story, while an illustration tells the story through a picture. Using a particular symbol or mood color to enhance the prose can provide a clearer meaning to the reader.

TEACHING
SUGGESTIONS: On a chalkboard, have students create a list of mood colors, and symbols, which can represent abstract feelings (e.g., a red heart, love). From this list, have students develop a storyline with an introduction, a body, a conflict and climax. Be sure students finish a storyline with a resolution. This is an excellent interdisciplinary activity for English and Art teachers. Once a storyline is developed, visual images will begin to form. These visual images should enhance the storyline and provide the storyline with a greater impact than the text alone.

35

**SUGGESTED
CLASSROOM
ACTIVITIES:**

When the storyline is in place, ask students to do preliminary sketches of their ideas. Encourage students to keep ideas simple, but, be sure students use symbols and mood colors. Once preliminary sketches have been drawn, have students begin to work on a computer with a graphics creative writing program. If students are not familiar with the graphics and creative writing program, be sure to provide students with ample instruction, demonstration and practice time. Be sure to discuss layout, word and image placement. Using the creative writing graphics package, images can be drawn and placed in various positions on the computer screen. Different programs offer a variety of type styles (fonts). Have students select a font which works well with their stories. Have students work until their storylines are complete with illustrations. It is a good idea to have students save their work in stages throughout the project.

**REINFORCEMENT
ACTIVITIES:**

Stories can be printed and then enhanced with appropriate colors. Use marker, watercolor or colored pencil to color hardcopies. Depending on the program, the disk images can be placed in sequence and viewed as a slide show. If printed in sequence, these images can be bound into books using one of several bookbinding techniques. For example, a hole punch may be used and yarn can be tied through the holes. Another alternative is to have a copy company do spiral binding. However, a fee is usually charged for this binding.

LESSON 13

Artistic Methods – Perspective

GRADE LEVEL: Grades 7 to 12

OBJECTIVE: Students will create a composition using linear perspective to convey space with shape and volume on a computer.

SUGGESTED INSTRUCTIONAL TIME: Five to ten 50 minute sessions (depending on age and complexity of assignments)

IMPORTANT TERMS: Linear perspective, Horizon line, One-point perspective, Two-point perspective, Volume

BACKGROUND: Perspective is a drawn interpretation of the perceptual effect of planes and volumes, indicating a direction in space. For example, as we look down a railroad track, into the distance, the track seems to converge to one point on the horizon line.

Drawings of buildings also demonstrate perspective. Building perspective may be at two points on the horizon line.

37

Two-point perspective can be seen in a building drawing which sets at the corner and has two sides visible to the viewer. Simple shapes, such as squares, can be developed to provide a sense of volume, by adding planes (sides).

Figure 1

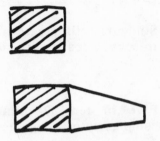

Depth created by the directional planes increases as the diagonals of the planes increase.

Figure 2

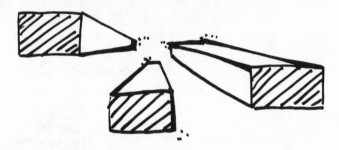

TEACHING SUGGESTIONS:

Consider using a tutorial program to teach perspective (e.g., "Art: Perspective Drawing"). This program, or one like it, can allow advanced students to move more quickly through the technical aspects of perspective. Likewise, such a program can allow slower students to progress at a rate which is more comfortable. Using this type of program can increase retention by practice, before students attempt the actual project. If possible, each student should be given the opportunity to work on a perspective tutorial program.

CLASSROOM ACTIVITIES:

Discuss and introduce the basic concepts of perspective. Have students sketch along as you demonstrate one- and two-point perspective, and creating volumes from shapes. Be sure to explain the objective of the lesson and show examples of finished work. Younger students may initially use only one eye-level, such as, above, at and below an object. Once students are capable of working at one eye-level, have students use multiple eye-level images at these different angles.

Above eye level   At eye level   Below eye level

Start with simple geometric shapes, such as rectangles or squares. Once these simple shapes become familiar, have students use cylinders and spheres for their designs. Color and texture may also be added. Allow students to continue until their designs are complete. Remind students to save their finished product on a disk.

REINFORCEMENT ACTIVITIES:

Once designs are complete, print out designs and have students add color, or photograph designs from the screen (see Design Elements, Lesson 3) and enlarge the photographs. Cardboard constructions of these volume designs may be built and attached to a base to create a three-dimensional sculpture. Backgounds may be painted to resemble space, and other shapes may be added to create a fantasy piece.

LESSON 14

Artistic Methods – Animation

GRADE LEVEL: Grades 7 to 9

OBJECTIVE: Using an animation program such as "Moviemaker," students will develop a simple animated sequence with one character and a background.

Characters should be able to move through space. In addition, student created characters should have animated detail, such as arms and legs.

SUGGESTED INSTRUCTIONAL TIME: Eight to ten 45 minute sessions

IMPORTANT TERMS: Each animation program for a computer is different. The process of actually creating animation is unique for each program, therefore, specific directions for creating computer animation will not be presented here. You will need to select and work with a program to master its functions and features. However, be sure to select a program appropriate for the age group that you will be teaching.

BACKGROUND: Any inanimate object cannot move, including drawings. However, if a series of several drawings, each with a slight change of position, are viewed in sequence at a certain rate of speed, the illusion of movement will appear. All animated actions are illusions because the movement does not actually take place. To create animation on film, artists draw many drawings for a very short length of movement. The use of a computer has an ability to reduce the actual number of drawn objects the artist must create to achieve the illusion of movement.

TEACHING SUGGESTIONS: Develop with students an understanding of how animation works and discuss several of the techniques of animation. It would be much easier to teach these concepts with film. Check with a media specialist or look through a 16 mm film catalog for a film on the how-to's of animation.

Information on how computer generated animation is used should also be provided to students. Most of the Saturday morning cartoon shows are now created on very sophisticated computers. Remind students they will not be able to duplicate these techniques with a microcomputer. However, students can create similar forms of animation.

Student animation will more closely resemble arcade games. Other uses of computer generated animation are the Monday Night Football introductions and the Home Box Office commercial, with its rotating logo. Remember, students should be shown a 16mm film on how the process of traditional animation is done. When students see the work involved in animating a single figure through drawing, they will appreciate the computer's capabilities.

Most microcomputer animation programs have several basic steps: drawing the figure, creating the background, and putting the two together in the proper sequence. Remember, actual steps in the process are dependent on the specific program. Make sure students have all the necessary steps, in handout form, for easy reference while they work. Work through the steps with the class before beginning the actual project.

CLASSROOM ACTIVITIES:

Have students try their hand at creating a simple flip book. The small note pads available at an office supply store will work for this project. Ask students to try something simple, such as a bouncing ball, or a car moving across the road. Work until the flip books are completed. Have students share their books with one another.

Introduce the computer project objective. Demonstrate an animation program. Be sure to hand out reference sheets listing computer functions and features. Show examples. While students work on their own projects, monitor their progress. Students should keep their characters simple for this experiment. Be certain to have students save their drawings on a disk, to be put into sequence, and run.

REINFORCEMENT ACTIVITIES:

Try shooting the sequences with a super 8 camera and 160 G film. A camera should be sophisticated enough to capture low light levels, with no room lights on. Ask students the following questions for discussion: How do the processes differ? What makes the computer characters differ from the hand drawn characters?

LESSON 15

Interior Design

GRADE LEVEL:

Grades 7 to 12

OBJECTIVE:

Students will create a floor plan using an interior design program. Once a floor plan has been created, students will be able to place furniture within their floor plan.

Students will select the inside of any type of building, such as, a movie theater, a grocery store, or a church, to design floor plans.

SUGGESTED INSTRUCTIONAL TIME:

Four to five 45 minute sessions, to work through a tutorial program (Floor Plan)

Four to five 45 minute sessions, to complete an actual interior layout

IMPORTANT TERMS:

Interior design, Floor plan, Traffic flow and Safety

BACKGROUND:

Interior design involves the inside planning of a building. All structures are designed by an architect and further developed by an interior designer. Often, an interior designer may work with an architect. In this lesson, students will plan architectural considerations, such as doorways and windows. In addition, students will decide where to place furniture in an interior. Interior design considerations include placing furniture to avoid people tripping, or sitting next to an air conditioning or heating unit. Taking furniture placement considerations into account, as well as other design considerations, such as peoples' movement through a store or comfort and visibility in a church, are all aspects of an interior designer's responsibilities.

"Floor Plan" is a computer program allowing for computer assisted room design and furniture arrangement. Other draw and paint programs may also be used for this project. Certain shapes can represent specific furniture. For example:

$\bigcirc$ = Table   ▭ = Sofa   △ =Lamp

43

A room may be created with simple rectangular arrangements or more complex designs. Each student should have their own work station.

TEACHING SUGGESTIONS:

Discuss the concepts of interior design. Be sure to discuss interior design, floor plan, traffic flow and safety considerations. For example, ask students what is an interior designer's function? Be sure to show examples of different interior designs from magazines.

CLASSROOM ACTIVITIES:

Have students complete a worksheet from a photo or sketch. Items on a worksheet should include: doors, closets, beds, tables, chairs and other pieces of furniture. For example:

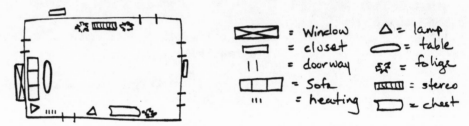

Ask students if the traffic flow workable for this particular type of room? Is there enough ventilation? Would the furniture work better in another arrangement? Have students sketch out changes they would make to improve the interior design. Once the paper worksheet is complete, introduce a computer project. Demonstrate a design program to be used. Be sure students have ample practice time to become familiar with the interior design program. Allow students to continue to work on their project. Remind students of traffic flow and safety concerns in their interior designs. Remind students to save finished projects on a disk.

REINFORCEMENT ACTIVITIES:

Print out student interior layouts. Using drapery, wallpaper, carpet and paint swatches (usually available from local retail stores), have students select a color scheme that will work for their interior designs. Explain to students that color can be used for specific room functions. For example, blues are cool and tend to make people work faster. Yellows are warm and tend to make people feel comfortable. Loud, large patterns tend to be hard to look at for long periods of time. Large graphic images such as arrows can be used to direct people through a building. Students should keep these principles in mind when selecting colors and patterns for their floor plan. Mount the swatches and floor plan on a cardboard base. Students may want to include pictures of furniture types with their interior designs.

LESSON 16

Artistic Methods – Commercial Design

GRADE LEVEL: Grades 11 to 12

OBJECTIVE: Students will create an original album cover using a computer and, if available, an image processor.

Photographic images may be combined with computer generated images to complete the design.

Students' completed work will be the standard album cover size for both the front and back cover.

SUGGESTED INSTRUCTIONAL TIME: Ten to fifteen 50 minute sessions

IMPORTANT TERMS: Layout, Text, Titles, Videodigitizing (image processing)

BACKGROUND: This is an advanced application of computerized image design. This project assumes some knowledge of image processing (see Design Principles, Lesson 10) and photographic techniques, such as Sabattier effect, high contrast or bas-relief. If students are unfamiliar with these concepts and skills, be sure to provide appropriate background. This lesson may be simplified by using the computer images alone, without the special effects of photographic techniques, high contrast or bas-relief.

TEACHING SUGGESTIONS: Introduce students to the layout process, the arrangement of words and visuals on an album cover. Bring in a variety of album covers to show the various uses of visuals and text.

Make sure students understand their finished product will be the same as an actual album cover. Students may wish to create images on the computer separately, print, enlarge or reduce on a photocopier, cutout and arrange on a cardboard base. Another option is to create the entire image on screen and enlarge and add color. If photographic capabilities are available, add the special effects.

CLASSROOM ACTIVITIES: Create a preliminary layout with text and visuals placement. Once preliminary work is completed, demonstrate the features of a draw/paint program. Try to choose a program which has a wide range of brush, color and special effects choices. Special effects included in a computer graphics program may include scaling to manipulate size, flipping of either part or all of the image, or zoom for detail work. Work closely with students, be sure to help students make creative decisions as they progress through the project. Allow students several practice sessions as they work through the concepts of image processing. Students should continue to work until designs are complete. Be certain that students save finished projects on a disk.

REINFORCEMENT ACTIVITIES:

Print out the design or parts of the design to be assembled. Allow students to add color with marker, layout films (Chartpak or Zipatone colors), watercolor or colored pencil. Students should use rubber cement to attach designs to a tagboard base. Make sure students include all of the aspects of the album design including titles, times, images, Universal Product Code (UPC) label, recording company logo and name, and any other important information. Remind students that all elements of their design should be original ideas. Students should not copy existing album covers. Finished covers may be laminated to give a professional, slick finish.

PART B
SOFTWARE DIRECTORY

CONCEPT: Animation
LEVEL: Grades 2 to 8
SOFTWARE TITLE: Low and Behold
PUBLISHER: Comp-Unique
                    4615 Clausen Ave.
                    Western Springs, IL 60558
SUGGESTED PRICE: $29.95
HARDWARE: Apple II Series
DESCRIPTION: Low and Behold is a low resolution graphics program that
                    allows students to draw straight and diagonal lines, boxes
                    and mirror images. Low and Behold also includes animation
                    and slide show features.

CONCEPT: Animation
LEVEL: Grades 3 to 6
SOFTWARE TITLE: A Child's Imagination
PUBLISHER: Spectrum Holobyte, Inc.
                    1050 Walnut St., Suite 525
                    Boulder, CO 80302
SUGGESTED PRICE: $49.95
HARDWARE: IBM PC, PCjr
DESCRIPTION: A Child's Imagination allows students to animate graphic
                    images. A database of images is provided or students can
                    create their own images.

CONCEPT: Animation
LEVEL: Grades 3 to 9
SOFTWARE TITLE: Professor Pixel
PUBLISHER: Individual Software, Inc.
                    1163 - I Chess Dr.
                    Foster City, CA 94404
SUGGESTED PRICE: $59.95
HARDWARE: IBM PC, Graphics Capability
DESCRIPTION: Professor Pixel instructs students in graphics, animation and
                    sound. This program uses BASIC programming language for
                    an interactive tutorial. In addition, Professor Pixel provides
                    instruction in graphic concepts, color, resolution, shading,
                    line, circles and arcs.

ANIMATION

CONCEPT: Animation
LEVEL: Grades 5 to 12
SOFTWARE TITLE: Spritemaster
PUBLISHER: Access Software
                           990 East 900 South
                           Salt Lake City, UT 84105
SUGGESTED PRICE: $39.95
HARDWARE: Commodore 64, Joystick
DESCRIPTION: With Spritemaster a user can draw images on a grid and then re-draw portions of the picture. Images can be animated and previewed. Changes in the picture can be viewed without affecting the stored images.
EVALUATION: *Softside*, November, 1983.

CONCEPT: Animation
LEVEL: Grades 5 to 12
SOFTWARE TITLE: Color-Craft
PUBLISHER: Sim Computer Products
                           P.O. Box 7
                           Miquon, PA 19452
SUGGESTED PRICE: $29.95
HARDWARE: Commodore 64 (64K); VIC 20 (16K)
DESCRIPTION: Color-Craft is an electronic palette. Students can create text or graphic symbols or combine text and graphics. Images can be displayed within a slide program. In addition, image display times can be controlled for use in animation.
EVALUATION: *InfoWorld*, October 24, 1983.

CONCEPT: Animation
LEVEL: Grades 6 to 12
SOFTWARE TITLE: Movie Maker
PUBLISHER: Reston Software, Prentice Hall, Inc.
                           11480 Suset Hills Rd.
                           Reston, VA 22090
SUGGESTED PRICE: $49.95
HARDWARE: Apple II Series; Atari 800XL, 1200XL; Commodore 64
DESCRIPTION: Movie Maker is an animation program allowing students to create short movies. Students begin by drawing shapes, adding background, then combining shapes into sequences and adding titles and special effects.
EVALUATION: *Classroom Computer Learning*, October, 1984.

CONCEPT: Animation
LEVEL: Grades 6 to 12
SOFTWARE TITLE: Mr. Pixel's Cartoon Kit
PUBLISHER: Mindscape, Inc.
                    3444 Dundee Rd.
                    Northbrook, IL 60062

SUGGESTED PRICE:
HARDWARE: Apple II Series; Commodore 64; IBM PC; Joystick
DESCRIPTION: Mr. Pixel's Cartoon Kit allows students to draw images, fill
                    color and animate characters. In addition, animated
                    characters can be made to interact.

CONCEPT: Animation
LEVEL: Grades 7 to 12
SOFTWARE TITLE: The Gibson Light Pen - PenPainter, PenDesigner,
                    PenAnimator
PUBLISHER: Koala Technologies
                    3100 Patrick Henry Dr.
                    Santa Clara, CA 95050
SUGGESTED PRICE: $199.00 (Apple); $99.00 (Commodore 64)
HARDWARE: Apple II Series; Commodore 64
DESCRIPTION: The Gibson Light Pen is a graphics design system that
                    allows students to interact directly on screen. Students can
                    draw and paint, draw free hand and animate their images.

CONCEPT: Animation
LEVEL: Grades 8 to 12
SOFTWARE TITLE: Graphicmaster
PUBLISHER: Tid Bit Software
                    P.O. Box 5579
                    Santa Barbara, CA 93018
SUGGESTED PRICE: $79.95
HARDWARE: Apple II Series; Apple III; Keyboard, Joystick, Paddles
DESCRIPTION: Graphicmaster has 5 interactive procedures for the creation
                    of text and animation.
EVALUATION: *Antic: The Atari Resource*, April, 1984; *Microcomputing*,
                    November, 1983.

ANIMATION

CONCEPT: Animation
LEVEL: Grades 9 to 12
SOFTWARE TITLE: GraForth
PUBLISHER: Insoft Corporation
                         10175 Barbor Blvd., Suite 202B
                         Portland, OR 97219
SUGGESTED PRICE: $75.00
HARDWARE: Apple II Series (48K)
DESCRIPTION: Images can be written in two and three dimensional
                         characters with GraForth. When images are in motion,
                         proportions remain exact. GraForth is also capable of
                         scaling and transformations.
EVALUATION: *Softside*, November, 1983.

CONCEPT: Animation
LEVEL: Grades 9 to 12
SOFTWARE TITLE: PM Animator
PUBLISHER: Don't Ask Computer Software
                         2265 Westwood Blvd., Suite B-150
                         Los Angeles, CA 90064
SUGGESTED PRICE: $44.95
HARDWARE: Atari 400, 800 (32K), BASIC, Joystick
DESCRIPTION: PM Animator allows the user to draw up to 16 frames of
                         images. These frames can then be saved and a second
                         group can be drawn and so on. A file editor is included for
                         easy animation splicing.
EVALUATION: *Softside*, November, 1983; *Creative Computing*, February,
                         1984.

CONCEPT: Animation
LEVEL: Grades 9 to 12
SOFTWARE TITLE: TAKE 1
PUBLISHER: Baudville Software
                         1001 Medical Park Dr. S.E.
                         Grand Rapids, MI 49506
SUGGESTED PRICE: $59.95
HARDWARE: Apple II Series
DESCRIPTION: Defining shapes and movements, frame-by-frame editing and
                         adding text is possible with TAKE 1. Also, scenes can be
                         combined to make "movies."

CONCEPT: Animation
LEVEL: Grades 9 to 12
SOFTWARE TITLE: A2-3D Graphics
PUBLISHER: Sublogic Corporation
                    713 Edgebrook Dr.
                    Champaign, IL 61820
SUGGESTED PRICE: $119.85
HARDWARE: Apple II Series (48K)
DESCRIPTION: A2-3D Graphics has a BASIC interface which allows the user
                    to place images into other BASIC programs. A user can
                    create and move three dimensional images and text. In
                    addition, special effects of a 2-3D Graphics include 3-D
                    movement and creation of 3-d text.
EVALUATION: *Popular Computing*, May, 1983.

CONCEPT: Animation
LEVEL: Grades 9 to 12
SOFTWARE TITLE: Graphics Magician
PUBLISHER: Penguin Software
                    P.O. Box 311
                    Geneva, IL 60134
SUGGESTED PRICE: $59.95
HARDWARE: Apple II Series; Apple III;
DESCRIPTION: Graphics Magician provides a set of editors and routines
                    designed to help create graphics and animation. Two
                    modules, the animation system and a picture system are used
                    to create shape and animation.
EVALUATION: *Creative Computing*, February, 1984; *Popular Computing*,
                    November, 1984.

CONCEPT: Animation
LEVEL: Grades 9 to 12
SOFTWARE TITLE: Artwork and Brushwork
PUBLISHER: Westend Film, Inc.
                    2121 Newport Pl. N. W.
                    Washington, DC 20037
SUGGESTED PRICE: $2,450.00 (Artwork), $1,450.00 (Brushwork)
HARDWARE: IBM PC (512K), DOS 2.0
DESCRIPTION: Artwork and Brushwork are high capacity graphics programs
                    which allow for video input. Features include drawing,
                    color shading, three dimensional shape manipulation,
                    animation and illustration of output features.
EVALUATION: *PC*, October 1, 1985.

CONCEPT: Draw and Paint
LEVEL: Grades K to 3
SOFTWARE TITLE: Magic Crayon
PUBLISHER: C and C Software
                    5713 Kentfield Circle
                    Wichita, KS 67220
SUGGESTED PRICE: $35.00
HARDWARE: Apple II Series (48K)
DESCRIPTION: Magic Crayon provides four levels of tutorial learning.
                    Topic levels include draw and design pictures and computer
                    usage. Each level differs in complexity for each topic.
EVALUATION: *InfoWorld*, October 17, 1983.

CONCEPT: Draw and Paint
LEVEL: Grades K to 7
SOFTWARE TITLE: Delta Drawing
PUBLISHER: Spinnaker Software, Inc.,
                    One Kendall Square
                    Cambridge, MA 02139
SUGGESTED PRICE: $39.95 - $49.95
HARDWARE: Apple II series; Atari; IBM PC, PCjr; Commodore 64
DESCRIPTION: Delta Drawing can be used to create computer graphics,
                    erase and move a picture around on the screen, and print
                    text. Delta drawing has single key commands for easy
                    student use.
EVALUATION: *The Atari Resource*, October, 1984.

CONCEPT: Draw and Paint
LEVEL: Grades 1 to 4
SOFTWARE TITLE: Computer Crayons
PUBLISHER: Futurehouse
                    P.O. Box 3470
                    Chapel Hill, NC 27514
SUGGESTED PRICE: $29.95 (Edumate Light Pen separately $34.95)
HARDWARE: Atari 400, 800 or XL Series; Commodore 64 with Edumate
                    Light Pen
DESCRIPTION: Computer Crayons is an alphabet and coloring book designed
                    to allow students practice in freehand sketching. A light
                    pen is used for direct screen freehand sketching.
                    Pre-designed art of each letter of the alphabet is provided.
EVALUATION: *Popular Computing*, October, 1984.

DRAW AND PAINT

CONCEPT: Draw and Paint
LEVEL: Grades 1 to 5
SOFTWARE TITLE: Picture Perfect
PUBLISHER: Methods and Solutions, Inc.
                        300 Unicorn Park Dr.
                        Woburn, MA 01801

SUGGESTED PRICE: $54.95
HARDWARE: Apple II Series (48K), Joystick or Mouse
DESCRIPTION: Picture Perfect allows students to create pictures and add text to their drawings. Students can draw free hand or use any of the 72 pre-designed shapes. These shapes include circles, rectangles, boxes and 69 other shapes.
EVALUATION: *InfoWorld*, October 15, 1984.

CONCEPT: Draw and Paint
LEVEL: Grades 1 to 5
SOFTWARE TITLE: Color Me: The Computer Coloring Kit
PUBLISHER: Mindscape, Inc.
                        3444 Dundee Rd.
                        Northbrook, IL 60062

SUGGESTED PRICE:
HARDWARE: Apple II Series; Commodore 64; Joystick
DESCRIPTION: Color Me: The Computer Coloring Book allows students to draw free hand or cut and paste pre-drawn characters. Students can then print out their pictures to make coloring books or stickers. Extra disk with additional pre-drawn pictures are available.

CONCEPT: Draw and Paint
LEVEL: Grades 1 to 5
SOFTWARE TITLE: Drawing Discovery
PUBLISHER: Trillium Press
                        P.O. Box 921 Madison Square Station
                        New York, NY 10159

SUGGESTED PRICE: $29.95
HARDWARE: Apple II Series
DESCRIPTION: Drawing Discovery allows students to draw and create their own pictures. Drawing Discovery can be used with a color or a monochrome monitor.

CONCEPT: Draw and Paint
LEVEL: Grades 1 to 5
SOFTWARE TITLE: Fingerpaint
PUBLISHER: Nova Software
                    P.O. Box 545
                    Alexandria, MN 56308
SUGGESTED PRICE: $34.95
HARDWARE: Apple II Series, Paddle or Joystick
DESCRIPTION: Fingerpaint is an "etch-a-sketch" that allows students to
                    simulate fingerpainting. Students can choose colors and
                    pre-designed images. A color book is provided which
                    includes material for free hand drawing.
EVALUATION: *Electronic Learning*, September, 1983.

CONCEPT: Draw and Paint
LEVEL: Grades 1 to 6
SOFTWARE TITLE: Pattern Maker
PUBLISHER: The Scarborough System
                    25 North Broadway
                    Tarrytown, NY 10591
SUGGESTED PRICE: $39.95
HARDWARE: Apple II Series (48K)
DESCRIPTION: Pattern Maker allows students to create a pattern using a
                    single keystroke. Once patterns are created, color can be
                    added. Patterns may be expanded or rotated. Pattern
                    Maker allows for the creation of tapestries, mosaics and
                    other pattern formats. An illustrated history of design and
                    student activities are included.
EVALUATION: *Booklist*, January, 1985.

CONCEPT: Draw and Paint
LEVEL: Grades 1 to 6
SOFTWARE TITLE: Micro-Painter
PUBLISHER: Datasoft, Inc.
                    19808 Nordhoff Pl.
                    Chatsworth, CA 91311
SUGGESTED PRICE: $34.95
HARDWARE: Atari, Apple II Series
DESCRIPTION: Micro-Painter allows students to use pre-designed images to
                    develop color designs. In addition, Micro-Painter allows
                    students to use 16 colors and 8 brightness levels.
EVALUATION: *Popular Computing*, October, 1984.

DRAW AND PAINT

CONCEPT: Draw and Paint
LEVEL: Grades 1 to 8
SOFTWARE TITLE: Picturewriter
PUBLISHER: Scarborough Systems
K-12 Micromedia
172 Broadway
Woodcliff Lake, NJ 07675
SUGGESTED PRICE: $39.95
HARDWARE: Apple II Series, Joystick
DESCRIPTION: Picturewriter allows students to store up to 64 different designs or images on disk. A tutorial is provided to guide students through the different functions of Picturewriter. Several features of Picturewriter include: 8 color choices, mixing of any two colors and pre-drawn images for student coloring or manipulation.
EVALUATION: *Booklist*, January 1, 1985.

CONCEPT: Draw and Paint
LEVEL: Grades 2 to 8
SOFTWARE TITLE: Low and Behold
PUBLISHER: Comp-Unique
4615 Clausen Ave.
Western Springs, IL 60558
SUGGESTED PRICE: $29.95
HARDWARE: Apple II Series
DESCRIPTION: Low and Behold is a low resolution graphics program that allows students to draw straight and diagonal lines, boxes and mirror images. Low and Behold also includes animation and slide show features.

CONCEPT: Draw and Paint
LEVEL: Grades 3 to 12
SOFTWARE TITLE: Koala Painter
PUBLISHER: Koala Technologies Corporation
3100 Patrick Henry Dr.
Santa Clara, CA 95052
SUGGESTED PRICE: $125.00 (Apple, IBM), $99.00 (Atari)
HARDWARE: Apple II Series; Atari 400, 800, XL series; IBM PC and PCjr
DESCRIPTION: Koala Painter is both a graphic tool and drawing program. Designs can be create, saved, edited and printed using this program. Koala Painter also allows pixel by pixel editing for detailed work.

CONCEPT: Draw and Paint
LEVEL: Grades 3 to 6
SOFTWARE TITLE: The Artist
PUBLISHER: Ksoft
                  845 Wellner Rd.
                  Naperville, IL 60540
SUGGESTED PRICE: $10.00
HARDWARE: Timex/Sinclair 1000 (16K)
DESCRIPTION: The Artist uses over 20 commands to create drawings and
                  paintings. Students can choose a variety of backgrounds for
                  their designs. The Artist allows students to mix graphics
                  and text.
EVALUATION: *Computers and Electronics*, December, 1982.

CONCEPT: Draw and Paint
LEVEL: Grades 3 to 12
SOFTWARE TITLE: Color Paint
PUBLISHER: IBM Corporation,
                  Educational Systems Business Unit
                  3715 Northside Pkwy
                  Atlanta, GA 30327
SUGGESTED PRICE: $99.00
HARDWARE: IBM PC, PCjr, PC XT; Mouse, DOS 2.1
DESCRIPTION: ColorPaint is a graphic design program which allows
                  students to draw free hand and use full color capabilities.
                  ColorPaint provides a choice of 16 colors, 30 patterns and a
                  number of brushes.
EVALUATION: *PC*, January 22, 1985.

CONCEPT: Draw and Paint
LEVEL: Grades 4 to 12
SOFTWARE TITLE: Doodle
PUBLISHER: City Software Distributors, Inc.,
                  735 W. Wisconsin Ave.
                  Milwaukee, WI 53233
SUGGESTED PRICE: $39.95
HARDWARE: Commodore 64, Joystick
DESCRIPTION: Doodle allows the user to draw pictures in 16 colors and
                  paint with 8 brush sizes. Negative or mirror images are
                  possible as well as the capability to enlarge, stretch or
                  rotate any part of an image.

DRAW AND PAINT

CONCEPT:	Draw and Paint
LEVEL:	Grades 4 to 12
SOFTWARE TITLE:	Mr. Pixel's Programming Paint Set
PUBLISHER:	Mindscape, Inc.
	3444 Dundee Rd.
	Northbrook, IL 60062
SUGGESTED PRICE:	
HARDWARE:	Apple II Series; Commodore 64; IBM PC; Joystick
DESCRIPTION:	With Mr. Pixel's Programming Paint Set, students can draw and paint, change colors, enlarge, repeat and relocate images or portions of images. Also, with Mr. Pixel's Programming Paint Set, students can develop programming skills.

CONCEPT:	Draw and Paint
LEVEL:	Grades 4 to 12
SOFTWARE TITLE:	MousePaint
PUBLISHER:	Apple Computer, Inc.
	20525 Mariani Ave.
	Cupertino, CA 95014
SUGGESTED PRICE:	$99.00
HARDWARE:	Apple IIe, IIc
DESCRIPTION:	MousePaint allows students to draw free hand graphics with a mouse. A mouse is provided with the software.

CONCEPT:	Draw and Paint
LEVEL:	Grades 4 to 12
SOFTWARE TITLE:	Roger's Easel
PUBLISHER:	Southwestern Data Systems
	P.O. Box 582
	Santee, CA 92071
SUGGESTED PRICE:	$24.95
HARDWARE:	Apple II, Paddles
DESCRIPTION:	Roger's Easel contains 3 programs including a sketching program. Pictures can be stored on a disk for recall at a later time.

CONCEPT: Draw and Paint
LEVEL: Grades 4 to 12
SOFTWARE TITLE: Magic Paintbrush
PUBLISHER: Penguin Software
                    P.O. Box 311
                    Geneva, IL 60134
SUGGESTED PRICE: $34.95
HARDWARE: Apple II Series; Commodore 64; IBM PC
DESCRIPTION: Magic Paintbrush is a drawing program which allows
                    students to create Hi Resolution pictures. Hi Resolution
                    pictures are created through the use of lines, circles and
                    brushes. Students can use clip art and pre-designs in
                    creating their own pictures.

CONCEPT: Draw and Paint
LEVEL: Grades 4 to 12
SOFTWARE TITLE: Dazzle Draw
PUBLISHER: Broderbund Software
                    2 Vista Wood Way
                    San Rafael, CA 94901
SUGGESTED PRICE: $59.95
HARDWARE: Apple IIe, IIc (128K)
DESCRIPTION: Dazzle Draw allows students to create drawings using up to
                    16 colored markers. In addition, various brushes and
                    patterns are provided for original work or editing
                    pre-designed images.
EVALUATION: *Byte*, March, 1985.

CONCEPT: Draw and Paint
LEVEL: Grades 4 to 12
SOFTWARE TITLE: Atari Graphics Composer
PUBLISHER: Versa Computing
                    3541 Old Conejo Rd., Suite 104
                    Newbury Park, CA 91320
SUGGESTED PRICE: $39.95
HARDWARE: Atari 400, 800, 1200XL, Keyboard or Joystick
DESCRIPTION: Atari Graphics Composer allows students to draw on a
                    Hi-Res screen. Once designs are created students can add
                    color to complete the design. In addition, Atari Graphics
                    Composer allows text to be added to a design.
EVALUATION: *Antic: The Atari Resource*, December, 1982.

61

DRAW AND PAINT

CONCEPT: Draw and Paint
LEVEL: Grades 4 to 12
SOFTWARE TITLE: Painter Power
PUBLISHER: Micro Lab
2699 Skokie Valley Rd.
Highland Park, IL 60035
SUGGESTED PRICE: $39.95
HARDWARE: Apple II Series, Paddles or Joystick
DESCRIPTION: Painter Power is a Hi-Res graphics program for creating pictures in 6 colors. A variety of brushes can be used to create original drawings. Users may also create brushes or use a pre-designed set of patterns.
EVALUATION: *Byte*, May, 1983.

CONCEPT: Draw and Paint
LEVEL: Grades 4 to 12
SOFTWARE TITLE: Beagle Graphics
PUBLISHER: Beagle Brothers Micro Software
4315 Sierra Vista
San Diego, CA 92103
SUGGESTED PRICE: $59.95
HARDWARE: Apple IIe (128K), IIc
DESCRIPTION: Beagle Graphics can be used to draw, cut and paste and fill or add text to a picture. All pictures can be condensed to conserve memory.

CONCEPT: Draw and Paint
LEVEL: Grades 4 to 12
SOFTWARE TITLE: Edu-Paint
PUBLISHER: San Juan School District
614 Sutter Ave.
Carmichael, CA 95608
SUGGESTED PRICE: $20.00
HARDWARE: Apple II Series, Joystick, Paddles or Tablet
DESCRIPTION: Edu-paint provides for rapid painting of pictures and shapes. A variety of colors and patterns are available.
EVALUATION: *Compute*, November, 1982.

CONCEPT: Draw and Paint
LEVEL: Grades 5 to 12
SOFTWARE TITLE: E-Z Draw 3.3
PUBLISHER: Sirius Software
                            10398 Rockingham Dr. #12
                            Sacramento, CA 95827
SUGGESTED PRICE: $39.95
HARDWARE: Apple II Series
DESCRIPTION: E-Z Draw allows students to produce freehand images using a keyboard. Six colors, mirroring, rotation and several text fonts are available for student use.
EVALUATION: *Popular Computing*, November, 1984.

CONCEPT: Draw and Paint
LEVEL: Grades 5 to 12
SOFTWARE TITLE: Color-Craft
PUBLISHER: Sim Computer Products
                            P.O. Box 7
                            Miquon, PA   19452
SUGGESTED PRICE: $29.95
HARDWARE: Commodore 64 (64K); VIC 20 (16K)
DESCRIPTION: Color-Craft is an electronic palette. Students can create text or graphic symbols or combine text and graphics. Images can be displayed within a slide program.   In addition, image display times can be controlled for use in animation.
EVALUATION: *InfoWorld*, October 24, 1983.

CONCEPT: Draw and Paint
LEVEL: Grades 5 to 12
SOFTWARE TITLE: Paint Magic
PUBLISHER: Data Most, Inc.
                            8943 Fullbright Ave.
                            Chatsworth, CA 91311
SUGGESTED PRICE: $49.95
HARDWARE: Commodore 64 (16K), Joystick
DESCRIPTION: Paint Magic is a draw and paint program that includes such functions as: draw, paint, transpose, grab, slide, merge, restore and shrink. Paint Magic provides a tutorial for self-instruction.
EVALUATION: *InfoWorld*, May 21, 1984.

DRAW AND PAINT

CONCEPT:	Draw and Paint
LEVEL:	Grades 5 to 12
SOFTWARE TITLE:	MacPaint
PUBLISHER:	Apple Computer, Inc.
	20525 Mariani Ave.
	Cupertino, CA 95104
SUGGESTED PRICE:	
HARDWARE:	MacIntosh
DESCRIPTION:	MacPaint allows students to custom design graphics and pictures using a mouse. Text may be added at a later time. (No color)
EVALUATION:	*PC*, January 22, 1985.

CONCEPT:	Draw and Paint
LEVEL:	Grades 5 to 12
SOFTWARE TITLE:	ES Painter
PUBLISHER:	E&S Software Services
	P.O. Box 238
	Bedford, MA 01730
SUGGESTED PRICE:	$45.00
HARDWARE:	IBM PC (64K), Joystick
DESCRIPTION:	Students can draw free hand and fill the picture with color using ES Painter.
EVALUATION:	*Popular Computing*, October, 1983.

CONCEPT:	Draw and Paint
LEVEL:	Grades 5 to 12
SOFTWARE TITLE:	Art and Graphics on the Apple II/IIe
PUBLISHER:	Wiley Professional Software
	605 Third Ave.
	New York, NY 10158
SUGGESTED PRICE:	$39.90
HARDWARE:	Apple II Series
DESCRIPTION:	Art and Graphics on the Apple allows students to create, store and recall drawings. Further, students can change the color, size or rotate the position of the image.

CONCEPT: Draw and Paint
LEVEL: Grades 6 to 12
SOFTWARE TITLE: Computer Palette
PUBLISHER: Edutek Corporation
                             415 Cambridge #4
                             Palo Alto, CA 94306
SUGGESTED PRICE: $25.00
HARDWARE: Apple II Series, Joystick, Paddles
DESCRIPTION: Computer Palette can be used to create designs or images in
                             16 different colors by using a joystick or paddles.

CONCEPT: Draw and Paint
LEVEL: Grades 6 to 12
SOFTWARE TITLE: U-Draw II
PUBLISHER: Muse Software
                             347 N. Charles St.
                             Baltimore, MD 21201
SUGGESTED PRICE:
HARDWARE: Apple II Series
DESCRIPTION: U-Draw II allows students to draw and manipulate
                             Hi-Resolution graphics on the screen. Images can be
                             expanded, moved and rotated with keyboard commands or
                             with program commands.

CONCEPT: Draw and Paint
LEVEL: Grades 6 to 12
SOFTWARE TITLE: PC Paint Brush
PUBLISHER: Z - Soft, International Microcomputer Software
                             633 5th Ave.
                             San Rafael, CA 94901
SUGGESTED PRICE: $139.00
HARDWARE: IBM PC (192K), DOS 2.0, Joystick or Mouse
DESCRIPTION: PC Paintbrush includes a color palette, texture patterns and
                             text. Students can draw free hand and re-arrange drawings
                             or a portion of the drawing.
EVALUATION: *PC Magazine*, January 8, 1985.

DRAW AND PAINT

CONCEPT: Draw and Paint
LEVEL: Grades 6 to 12
SOFTWARE TITLE: Blazing Paddles
PUBLISHER: Baudville
                    1001 Medical Park Dr. S.E.
                    Grand Rapids, MI 49506
SUGGESTED PRICE: $49.95 Apple; $34.95 Commodore
HARDWARE: Apple II Series; Commodore 64; Joystick, light pen or mouse
DESCRIPTION: Blazing Paddles provides color mixing to create over 200
                    textured hues. Text fonts and pre-drawn shapes are
                    included, in addition to airbrush and other brush strokes
                    and pixel by pixel editing.

CONCEPT: Draw and Paint
LEVEL: Grades 6 to 12
SOFTWARE TITLE: Professor Pixel
PUBLISHER: Individual Software, Inc.
                    1163 - I Chess Dr.
                    Foster City, CA 94404
SUGGESTED PRICE: $59.95
HARDWARE: IBM PC, graphics capability
DESCRIPTION: Professor Pixel instructs students in graphics, animation and
                    sound. This program uses BASIC programming language for
                    an interactive tutorial. In addition, Professor Pixel provides
                    instruction in graphic concepts, color, resolution, shading,
                    line, circles and arcs.

CONCEPT: Draw and Paint
LEVEL: Grades 7 to 12
SOFTWARE TITLE: Electroboard Graphics
PUBLISHER: Monument Computer Service
                    P.O. Box 603
                    Joshua Tree, CA 92252
SUGGESTED PRICE: $200.00
HARDWARE: Apple II Series, (64K)
DESCRIPTION: Electroboard Graphics allows students to draw images and
                    create text displays. Electroboard Graphics also allows
                    students to combine images and animate drawings.

CONCEPT: Draw and Paint
LEVEL: Grades 7 to 12
SOFTWARE TITLE: Superdraw
PUBLISHER: Classroom Consortia Media, Inc.
                    57 Bay St.
                    Staten Island, NY 10301
SUGGESTED PRICE: $195.00
HARDWARE: IBM PC (128K), IBM PC AT, IBM PCjr (128K)
DESCRIPTION: Superdraw allows students to create designs using circles,
                    shapes, mirror images and color. Color can be used for
                    shading. Students can enlarge sections for greater precision
                    and detail. In addition, Superdraw allows the use of a
                    variety of fonts.

CONCEPT: Draw and Paint
LEVEL: Grades 8 to 12
SOFTWARE TITLE: A.G.I.L. Paint Program
PUBLISHER: Animation Graphics, Inc.
                    11317 Sunset Hills Rd.
                    Reston, VA 22090
SUGGESTED PRICE: $35.00
HARDWARE: Apple II+, IIe Keyboard or Joystick
DESCRIPTION: A.G.I.L. uses a variety of pens, fonts and shapes to create
                    text, geometric shapes and two page animation.

CONCEPT: Draw and Paint
LEVEL: Grades 8 to 12
SOFTWARE TITLE: PC Paint
PUBLISHER: Mouse Systems
                    23364 Walsh Ave.
                    Santa Clara, CA 95051
SUGGESTED PRICE: $99.00
HARDWARE: IBM PC (256K), DOS 2.X, Mouse, color monitor
DESCRIPTION: PC Paint is a draw and paint program with 6 palettes, each
                    with 3 colors. A number of brushes including a spray paint
                    brush are available.
EVALUATION: *PC Magazine*, October 1, 1985.

DRAW AND PAINT

CONCEPT:	Draw and Paint
LEVEL:	Grade 9 to 12
SOFTWARE TITLE:	Easel
PUBLISHER:	Time Arts, Inc.
	4425 Cavedale Rd.
	GlenEllyn, CA 95442
SUGGESTED PRICE:	$625.00
HARDWARE:	IBM PC, Color Monitor
DESCRIPTION:	Easel allows the user to draw and paint, create special brushes, vary the tints of chosen colors, scale drawings and put images into perspective. Easel also allows shaping, tilting and rotating of images. In addition, Easel has video digitizing capabilities.
EVALUATION:	*Creative Computing*, February, 1984.

CONCEPT:	Draw and Paint
LEVEL:	Grade 9 to 12
SOFTWARE TITLE:	Videogram
PUBLISHER:	Softel, Inc.,
	34 1/2 St. Mark's Place
	New York, NY 10003
SUGGESTED PRICE:	$200.00
HARDWARE:	IBM PC (512K), DOS 3.0; IBM EGA (256K)
DESCRIPTION:	Videogram is a mid-range graphics program which includes 64 colors and 42 text fonts. Special features include cut and paste, superimposing of images and enlarging areas of images for detail work. Videogram also has a slide-show function.
EVALUATION:	*PC Magazine*, October 1, 1985.

CONCEPT:	Draw and Paint
LEVEL:	Grades 9 to 12
SOFTWARE TITLE:	Alpha Plot
PUBLISHER:	Beagle Brothers Micro Software
	4315 Sierra Vista
	San Diego, CA 92103
SUGGESTED PRICE:	$39.50
HARDWARE:	Apple II Series, Keyboard, Joystick or Paddles
DESCRIPTION:	Alpha Plot allows the user to draw and paint images, move sections, superimpose or reverse the images. Lines can be viewed before entering onto the picture.

CONCEPT: Draw and Paint
LEVEL: Grades 3 to 8
SOFTWARE TITLE: Videographs
PUBLISHER: Texas Instruments, Inc.,
                            P.O. Box 53
                            Lubbock, TX 79408
SUGGESTED PRICE: $19.95
HARDWARE: TI 99/4A
DESCRIPTION: With Videographs it is easy to create original images, rework pre-designed pictures or create new patterns.
EVALUATION: *Popular Computing*, November, 1983.

CONCEPT: Draw and Paint
LEVEL: Grades 8 to 12
SOFTWARE TITLE: Art Gallery
PUBLISHER: Radio Shack
                            1800 One Tandy Center
                            Fort Worth, TX 76102
SUGGESTED PRICE: $39.95
HARDWARE: TRS-80
DESCRIPTION: Art Gallery allows the user to create original pictures. Some of the features include: cursor control, picture size control, draw and paint commands, alpha-numeric type set and text scrolling. With the pre-programmed pictures, Art Gallery can also be used as an electronic coloring book, if desired.

CONCEPT: Draw and Paint
LEVEL: Grades 6 to 12
SOFTWARE TITLE: Joypaint 1.1
PUBLISHER: Pcomputer Pictures
                            53 Sherman Ave.
                            Rockville Center, NY 11570
SUGGESTED PRICE: $49.95
HARDWARE: IBM PC, 64K, DOS 1.1, Color Adapter, Game Adapter, Two Button Joystick
DESCRIPTION: Joypaint 1.1 can be used to create full page graphics using a variety of brushes and brush sizes. Full or split screen use is available with 16 available colors. Joypaint 1.1 also allows for image reduction, flipping and magnifying images.
EVALUATION: *Softside*, November, 1983.

DRAW AND PAINT

CONCEPT: Draw and Paint
LEVEL: Grades 4 to 12
SOFTWARE TITLE: Paint
PUBLISHER: Reston Publishing Co.
                    11480 Sunset Hills Rd.
                    Reston, VA 22090
SUGGESTED PRICE: $39.95
HARDWARE: Atari 800, 48K, Keyboard or Joystick
DESCRIPTION: Paint provides three menu choices: Simple Paint for easy or
                    simple drawings and limited brushes and colors; Super Paint
                    provides 81 brushes and many colors and special controls;
                    and Art Show for displaying stored pictures. Instructors
                    manual includes a chapter on Art History and a chapter on
                    computer graphics applications.
EVALUATION: *Popular Computing*, November, 1983; *Electronic Learning*,
                    October, 1982.

CONCEPT: Draw and Paint
LEVEL: Grades 4 to 12
SOFTWARE TITLE: Video Easel
PUBLISHER: Atari Home Computer Division
                    P. O. Box 61657
                    Sunnyvale, CA 94086
SUGGESTED PRICE: $34.95
HARDWARE: Atari 400, 800, 1200XL, Keyboard or Joystick
DESCRIPTION: Video Easel allows users to create colored designs, line
                    drawing and brush simulation. The computer can add to the
                    designs to assist in teaching the relationship between color
                    and design.
EVALUATION: *Popular Computing*, November, 1983.

CONCEPT: Draw and Paint
LEVEL: Grades K to 5
SOFTWARE TITLE: Micro Painter
PUBLISHER: Datasoft Inc.,
                    9421 Winnetka Ave.
                    Chatsworth, CA 91311
SUGGESTED PRICE: $34.95
HARDWARE: Atari 400, 800, 1200XL; TRS-80
DESCRIPTION: Micro Painter does not allow actual drawing but provides
                    preprogrammed outlines for coloring and painting by
                    numbers. Micro Painter is essentially an electronic coloring
                    book.

CONCEPT: Draw and Paint
LEVEL: Grades 4 to 12
SOFTWARE TITLE: Sketchpad
PUBLISHER: Atari Program Exchange
                        P. O. Box 30705
                        Santa Clara, CA 95055
SUGGESTED PRICE: $24.95
HARDWARE: Atari 400, 800, 1200XL, Keyboard or Joystick
DESCRIPTION: Sketchpad allows the user to draw circles, rectangles, points
                        and other design elements. The user can also draw, paint
                        and combine designs. Sketchpad is limited to 4 colors at
                        one time.

CONCEPT: Draw and Paint
LEVEL: Grades 4 to 12
SOFTWARE TITLE: Flying Colors
PUBLISHER: The Computer Colorworks
                        330 Bridgeway
                        Sausalito, CA 94965
SUGGESTED PRICE: $39.95
HARDWARE: Apple II Series, Graphics tablet, Joystick
DESCRIPTION: Flying Colors is an interactive program with high resolution
                        capabilities. Flying Colors allows the user to draw or paint
                        anywhere on the screen with adjustable cursor speed and
                        several brushes.
EVALUATION: *Creative Computing*, February, 1984; *Softtalk*, March, 1984;
                        Educational Technology, September, 1984.

CONCEPT: Draw and Paint
LEVEL: Grades 7 to 12
SOFTWARE TITLE: Action Art
PUBLISHER: Classroom Consortia Media, Inc.
                        57 Bay St.
                        Staten Island, NY 10301
SUGGESTED PRICE: $69.95
HARDWARE: IBM PC (128K), PC XT, PC AT, PCjr,
DESCRIPTION: Action Art Allows students to draw programs using a variety
                        of colors and shading. Action Art also lets students create
                        circles, triangles and other polygons.

DRAW AND PAINT

CONCEPT:	Draw and Paint
LEVEL:	Grades 7 to 12
SOFTWARE TITLE:	The Gibson Light Pen - PenPainter, PenDesigner, PenAnimator
PUBLISHER:	Koala Technologies 3100 Patrick Henry Dr. Santa Clara, CA 95050
SUGGESTED PRICE:	$199.00 (Apple); $99.00 (Commodore 64)
HARDWARE:	Apple II Series; Commodore 64
DESCRIPTION:	The Gibson Light Pen is a graphics design system that allows students to interact directly on screen. Students can draw and paint, draw free hand or animate their images.

CONCEPT:	Draw and Paint
LEVEL:	Grades 9 to 12
SOFTWARE TITLE:	The Complete Graphics System
PUBLISHER:	Penguin Software P.O. Box 311 Geneva, IL 60134
SUGGESTED PRICE:	$79.95
HARDWARE:	Apple II Series; Apple III; Keyboard, Joystick, Paddles
DESCRIPTION:	The Complete Graphics System provides for free hand drawing as well as the use of pre-designed geometric shapes. Over 100 colors and 96 brushes are available. Special effects such as zoom, flip, scale and rotation of three dimensional shapes are also available.
EVALUATION:	*Popular Computing*, November, 1984.

CONCEPT:	Draw and Paint
LEVEL:	Grades 9 to 12
SOFTWARE TITLE:	Peripheral Vision
PUBLISHER:	Future House P.O. Box 3470 Chapel Hill, NC 27514
SUGGESTED PRICE:	$59.95 (with Edumate light pen)
HARDWARE:	Atari 400, 800 or XL series; Commodore 64 with Edumate light pen
DESCRIPTION:	Peripheral Vision allows students to sketch on the computer and make color or design changes of sketches. Images created through Peripheral Vision can be incorporated with other programs. Pre-designed shapes, mirroring, and zoom are features to use with any of 35 two-color patterns and textures to manipulate images.
EVALUATION:	*Popular Computing*, October, 1984.

CONCEPT: Draw and Paint
LEVEL: Grades 9 to 12
SOFTWARE TITLE: The Coloring Book
PUBLISHER: Software Tech For Computers
                      P.O. Box 428
                      Belmont, MA 02178
SUGGESTED PRICE: $60.00
HARDWARE: Apple II Series (48K), Joystick or Paddles
DESCRIPTION: The Coloring Book provides students with freehand drawing
                      capabilities. Text may be added to drawings in several
                      different colors.

CONCEPT: Draw and Paint
LEVEL: Grades 9 to 12
SOFTWARE TITLE: Paintmaster
PUBLISHER: Avant-Garde Creations
                      P.O. Box 30160
                      Eugene, OR 97403
SUGGESTED PRICE: $34.95
HARDWARE: Apple II Series, Joystick
DESCRIPTION: Paintmaster provides students with a choice of freehand or
                      geometric drawings.   Up to 32 colors are available at any
                      one time for student use.
EVALUATION: *Popular Computing*, November, 1984.

CONCEPT: Draw and Paint
LEVEL: Grades 9 to 12
SOFTWARE TITLE: Lumena
PUBLISHER: Time Arts, Inc.
                      3436 Mendecino Ave.
                      Santa Rosa, CA 95401
SUGGESTED PRICE: $495.00
HARDWARE: Mindset, Graphics Tablet
DESCRIPTION: Lumena allows students to design, store and retrieve graphic
                      images. Scaling, rotation and animation are features of
                      Lumena. Lumena is a mid-range graphics system with
                      higher-end sophistication.
EVALUATION: *Creative Computing*, February, 1985.

DRAW AND PAINT

CONCEPT: Draw and Paint
LEVEL: Grades 9 to 12
SOFTWARE TITLE: Graphics Processing System
PUBLISHER: Stoneware, Inc.
                     50 Belvedere St.
                     San Rafael, CA 94901
SUGGESTED PRICE: $99.95
HARDWARE: Apple II (48K), Joystick, Paddles or Graphics Tablet
DESCRIPTION: Graphics Processing System allows students to create free
                     hand or line drawings. Color, fill, size modification and
                     zoom are available functions. In addition, text can be added
                     to drawings.
EVALUATION: *MicroComputing*, March, 1983.

CONCEPT: Draw and Paint
LEVEL: Grades 9 to 12
SOFTWARE TITLE: Artwork and Brushwork
PUBLISHER: Westend Film, Inc.
                     2121 Newport Pl. N.W.
                     Washington, D.C. 20037
SUGGESTED PRICE: $2,450.00 (Artwork), $1,450.00 (Brushwork)
HARDWARE: IBM PC (512K), DOS 2.0
DESCRIPTION: Artwork and Brushwork are high capacity graphics programs
                     which allow for video input. Features include drawing,
                     color shading, three dimensional shape manipulation,
                     animation and illustration of output features.
EVALUATION: *PC*, October 1, 1985.

CONCEPT: Draw and Paint
LEVEL: Grades 9 to 12
SOFTWARE TITLE: Imigit
PUBLISHER: Chorus Data Systems, Inc.
                     P.O. Box 370, 6 Continental Blvd.
                     Merrimack, NH 03054
SUGGESTED PRICE: $295.00; Imigit Plus $695.00
HARDWARE: IBM PC (256K)
DESCRIPTION: Imigit is a 16 color (256 colors for Imigit Plus) graphics
                     creation program. Imigit has the capability of capturing
                     video images for manipulation in editing. Student created
                     images can be overlayed, or combined with other images.
EVALUATION: *PC*, October 1, 1985.

CONCEPT: Draw and Paint
LEVEL: Grades 9 to 12
SOFTWARE TITLE: PC Draw
PUBLISHER: Micro Grafx
                    1701 North Greenville Ave. Suite 703
                    Richardson, TX 75081
SUGGESTED PRICE: $295.00
HARDWARE: IBM PC, PC XT
DESCRIPTION: PC Draw is a drawing system with symbol libraries, software design, electronics design and alternative text. Multiple text fonts and the capability to design student fonts is available. Functions include: scale, rotate and placement.
EVALUATION: *PC*, June 11, 1985.

CONCEPT: Draw and Paint
LEVEL: Grades 9 to 12
SOFTWARE TITLE: Dr. Halo
PUBLISHER: Media Cybernetics
                    7042 Carroll Ave.
                    Takoma Park, MD 20912
SUGGESTED PRICE: $99.95
HARDWARE: IBM PC (256K)
DESCRIPTION: Dr. Halo allows students to create designs with color and pattern palettes. In addition, eight typefaces in five sizes, rotation of images or of the entire screen are available.
EVALUATION: *PC Magazine*, January 8, 1985.

CONCEPT: Draw and Paint
LEVEL: Grades 9 to 12
SOFTWARE TITLE: Artist Designer II
PUBLISHER: Apple Computer Co.
                    10260 Bandley Dr.
                    Cupertino, CA 95014
SUGGESTED PRICE: $75.00
HARDWARE: Apple II Series (48K)
DESCRIPTION: Artist Designer II allows students to draw or paint using 5 colors. Tints, shades and color mixtures can be used by mixing colors with black and white. With Artist Designer II, students can see the step by step creation of their drawing and make a slide show presentation.

DRAW AND PAINT

CONCEPT: Draw and Paint
LEVEL: Grades 9 to 12
SOFTWARE TITLE: Graphic Tablet System
PUBLISHER: Apple Computer Co.
                             10260 Bandley Dr.
                             Cupertino, CA 95014
SUGGESTED PRICE: $75.00
HARDWARE: Apple II Series (48K), Graphics Tablet
DESCRIPTION: The Graphics Tablet System allows students to create pictures through a variety of modes using 64 color options and 40 brushes. Students can also create animation with Artist Designer II.

CONCEPT: Draw and Paint
LEVEL: Grades 9 to 12
SOFTWARE TITLE: Graphix Partner
PUBLISHER: Brightbill - Roberts, Ltd.
                             120 E. Washington St. Suite 421 Univ Bldg.
                             Syracuse, NY 13202
SUGGESTED PRICE: $149.00 (including Plotter Partner)
HARDWARE: IBM PC
DESCRIPTION: Graphix Partner allows students to create their own free hand drawings or use a variety of pre-designed images. Graphix Partner also includes 20 type styles and a variety of patterns that can be merged.
EVALUATION: *PC Week*, September, 11 1984; *PC Magazine*, October 1, 1985.

CONCEPT: Draw and Paint
LEVEL: Grades 9 to 12
SOFTWARE TITLE: The Digital Paintbrush System
PUBLISHER: The Computer Colorworks/Jandel Scientific
                             3030 Bridgeway
                             Saulsalito, CA 94965
SUGGESTED PRICE: $299.00
HARDWARE: Apple II Series; IBM PC, IBM PC XT
DESCRIPTION: The Digital Paintbrush System allows students to draw free hand, trace design layouts, create charts and make measurements. This print program has a variety of color palettes and brush choices.

CONCEPT: Draw and Paint
LEVEL: Grades 9 to 12
SOFTWARE TITLE: Graphics for the Apple
PUBLISHER: Kern International, Inc.
 433 Washington St., P.O. Box 1029
 Duxbury, MA 02332
SUGGESTED PRICE: $21.50
HARDWARE: Apple II Series
DESCRIPTION: Graphics for the Apple is a collection of 67 programs for two and three dimensional graphics. Graphics for the Apple includes software for the interactive creation of drawings.

CONCEPT: Draw and Paint
LEVEL: Grades 9 to 12
SOFTWARE TITLE: 4 - Point Graphics
PUBLISHER: IMSI
 633 Fifth Ave.
 San Rafael, CA 94901
SUGGESTED PRICE: $195.00
HARDWARE: IBM PC (128K)
DESCRIPTION: With 4 - Point Graphics, students can draw circles, ellipses, straight lines or rectangles with a keyboard. Drawings can be filled with color or the color can be changed. In addition, text can be added and the drawings can be moved or animated.
EVALUATION: *Whole Earth Software Catalog*, 1984.

CONCEPT: Draw and Paint
LEVEL: Grades 9 to 12
SOFTWARE TITLE: Graphics for the IBM PC
PUBLISHER: Kern International, Inc.
 433 Washington St., P.O. Box 1029
 Duxbury, MA 02332
SUGGESTED PRICE: $21.50
HARDWARE: IBM PC
DESCRIPTION: Graphics for the IBM PC is a collection of 67 programs for two and three dimensional graphics. Graphics for the IBM PC includes software for the interactive creation of drawings.

DRAW AND PAINT

CONCEPT: Draw and Paint
LEVEL: Grades 9 to 12
SOFTWARE TITLE: 3-D Computer Graphics: Perspective Drawing with the
                    Computer
PUBLISHER: Entelek, Ward-Whidden House
                    The Hill, P.O. Box 1303
                    Portsmouth, NH 03801
SUGGESTED PRICE: $75.00
HARDWARE: Apple IIe
DESCRIPTION: With 3-D Computer Graphics, students can generate shapes,
                    learn perspective drawing and manipulate objects in space.
                    Other options include picture construction, advanced
                    projection and three dimensional images.

CONCEPT: Graphic Utility
LEVEL: Grades K to 5
SOFTWARE TITLE: Rainbow Printer
PUBLISHER: Springboard Software
                  Rainbow Painter
                  Charles Clark Co., Inc.
                  168 Express Dr. South
                  Brentwood, NY   11717
SUGGESTED PRICE: $34.95
HARDWARE: Apple II Series; Commodore 64; IBM PCjr
DESCRIPTION: Rainbow Printer allows students to choose from a series of pictures for coloring. This program also allows students and teachers to create pictures through use of 50 brushes and color patterns. Rainbow Printer can be used to develop fine motor skills in students.

CONCEPT: Graphic Utility
LEVEL: Grades K to 5
SOFTWARE TITLE: Mask Parade
PUBLISHER: Springboard Software
                  Charles Clark Co., Inc.
                  168 Express Dr. South
                  Brentwood, NY   11717
SUGGESTED PRICE: $39.95
HARDWARE: Apple II Series (48K); Commodore 64; IBM PC
DESCRIPTION: Mask Parade is a program that allows young children to design their own mask, hats, glasses, etc. Predesigned or original works can be used.

CONCEPT: Graphic Utility
LEVEL: Grades 3 to 5
SOFTWARE TITLE: Koala Painter
PUBLISHER: Koala Technologies Corporation
                  3100 Patrick Henry Dr.
                  Santa Clara, CA 95052
SUGGESTED PRICE: $125.00 (Apple, IBM), $99.00 Atari
HARDWARE: Apple II Series; Atari 400, 800, XL Series; IBM PC and PCjr
DESCRIPTION: Koala Painter is both a graphic tool and drawing program. Designs can be created, saved, edited and printed using this program.

GRAPHIC UTILITY

CONCEPT: Graphic Utility
LEVEL: Grades 3 to 9
SOFTWARE TITLE: The Art Studio
PUBLISHER: Spectrum Holobyte, Inc.
                    1050 Walnut, Suite 325
                    Boulder, CO 80302
SUGGESTED PRICE: $49.95
HARDWARE: IBM PC, PCjr, XT, AT (128K) Color Graphics Adaptor;
                    Mouse or Tablet; DOS 2.0 or higher
DESCRIPTION: The Art Studio uses a mouse or graphics tablet to create
                    designs using boxes and lines. Custom brushes and text
                    fonts are available to create detail in student designs.

CONCEPT: Graphic Utility
LEVEL: Grades 4 to 12
SOFTWARE TITLE: Poster
PUBLISHER: Springboard Software
                    Charles Clark Co. Inc.
                    168 Express Drive South
                    Brentwood, NY 11717
SUGGESTED PRICE: $29.95
HARDWARE: Apple II Series; Commodore 64; IBM PC, PCjr
DESCRIPTION: Poster allows students to create colorful graphic images. As
                    students create images, students learn common programming
                    techniques. In addition, Poster has story telling capabilities.

CONCEPT: Graphic Utility
LEVEL: Grades 4 to 12
SOFTWARE TITLE: Graphiti Is Yours
PUBLISHER: Micro Power and Light Co.
                    12820 Hillcrest Rd. #224
                    Dallas, TX 75230
SUGGESTED PRICE: $29.95
HARDWARE: Apple II Series
DESCRIPTION: Graphiti Is Yours is a graphics package designed by a
                    teacher to provide for Hi-Resolution graphics for classroom
                    use. Drawings can be saved on a disk for later use.

CONCEPT: Graphic Utility
LEVEL: Grades 4 to 12
SOFTWARE TITLE: Graphics Exhibitor
PUBLISHER: Koala Technologies
                     4962 El Camino Real, Ste 125
                     Los Altos, CA 94022
SUGGESTED PRICE: $39.95
HARDWARE: Apple II Series
DESCRIPTION: Graphics Exhibitor provides the capability to create, modify, label and print designs made on a Koala Pad. Designs can be exhibited in a slide show format.

CONCEPT: Graphic Utility
LEVEL: Grades 5 to 12
SOFTWARE TITLE: Graphx
PUBLISHER: Graphx
                     P.O. Box C, 568 Clarence St.
                     Sydney, NSW Australia 2000
SUGGESTED PRICE: $50.00
HARDWARE: TI-99/4A, Joystick
DESCRIPTION: Graphx is a screen graphics program as well as a printing utility for designing banners, posters and other designs. Images can be animated.
EVALUATION: *Home Computer Magazine,* Vol.5, 1985.

CONCEPT: Graphic Utility
LEVEL: Grades 5 to 12
SOFTWARE TITLE: Visualizer
PUBLISHER: Maximus, Inc.
                     6723 Whitter Ave.
                     McLean, VA 22101
SUGGESTED PRICE: $49.95
HARDWARE: Atari 800, 1200, Atari Program Recorder
DESCRIPTION: Visualizer is a graphics management system that allows students to use color animation, display text and add audio soundtrack to graphic creations. Visualizer also has slide show capabilities.

GRAPHIC UTILITY

CONCEPT: Graphic Utility
LEVEL: Grades 6 to 12
SOFTWARE TITLE: Super Slide Show
PUBLISHER: Animation Graphics, Inc.
                     11317 Sunset Hills Rd.
                     Reston, VA 22090
SUGGESTED PRICE: $29.00
HARDWARE: Apple II+, IIe
DESCRIPTION: Super Slide Show allows the user to put together pictures
                     created on an Apple into a slide show.
EVALUATION: *Micro*, October, 1982.

CONCEPT: Graphic Utility
LEVEL: Grades 6 to 12
SOFTWARE TITLE: The Graphics Kit
PUBLISHER: Softsync, Inc.
                     14 East 34th St.
                     New York, NY 10016
SUGGESTED PRICE: $14.95
HARDWARE: Timex/Sinclair 1000 (16K)
DESCRIPTION: The Graphics Kit allows students to create shapes using
                     characters or geometrical shapes.
EVALUATION: *Micro Computing*, June, 1983; *Popular Computing*, March,
                     1984.

CONCEPT: Graphic Utility
LEVEL: Grades 6 to 12
SOFTWARE TITLE: Paper Graphics
PUBLISHER: Penguin Software
                     P.O. Box 311
                     Geneva, IL 60134
SUGGESTED PRICE: $49.95
HARDWARE: Apple II Series
DESCRIPTION: Paper Graphics is a program that will transfer Hi-Resolution
                     graphics from a screen to a dot matrix printer. Paper
                     Graphics allows students to reduce, magnify, reverse or add
                     text to images to be printed.

CONCEPT: Graphic Utility
LEVEL: Grades 6 to 12
SOFTWARE TITLE: The Print Shop
PUBLISHER: Broderbund Software
 17 Paul Dr.
 San Rafael, CA 94903
SUGGESTED PRICE: $49.95
HARDWARE: Apple II Series; Atari; Commodore 64
DESCRIPTION: The Print shop allows the user to write a story, design and paint an original design, make signs, banners and invitations. Many designs are provided on disk for use with The Print Shop.
EVALUATION: *Computing Teacher*, February, 1985; *Infoworld*, April 23, 1984.

CONCEPT: Graphic Utility
LEVEL: Grades 6 to 12
SOFTWARE TITLE: The Print Shop Companion, Print Shop Graphics Library (Update Programs)
PUBLISHER: Broderbund Software
 17 Paul Dr.
 San Rafael, CA 94903
SUGGESTED PRICE: $44.95 - $49.95
HARDWARE: Apple II Series (48K); Commodore 64; Koala Pad; Joystick; Printer
DESCRIPTION: The Print Shop Companion includes updated programs for creating signs, banners, letterheads and posters. This program provides additional selection graphics and fonts for The Print Shop.
EVALUATION: *The Computing Teacher*, February, 1985.

CONCEPT: Graphic Utility
LEVEL: Grades 8 to 12
SOFTWARE TITLE: Sprite Designer
PUBLISHER: Academy Software
 P. O. Box 9403
 San Rafael, CA 94912
SUGGESTED PRICE: $21.95
HARDWARE: Commodore 64
DESCRIPTION: Sprite Designer can be used to reduce or elongate horizontally or vertically any sprite designed with this program. Further, sprites can be merged, reversed, rotated, reflected and translated with this program.
EVALUATION: *Computing Teacher*, March, 1984.

GRAPHIC UTILITY

CONCEPT: Graphic Utility
LEVEL: Grades 9 to 12
SOFTWARE TITLE: A2-3D Graphics
PUBLISHER: Sublogic Corporation
                           713 Edgebrook Dr.
                           Champaign, IL 61820
SUGGESTED PRICE: $119.85
HARDWARE: Apple II Series, (48K), DOS 3.3
DESCRIPTION: A2-3D Graphics has a BASIC interface which allows the user to place images into other BASIC programs. A user can create and move three dimensional images, including movement and text.

CONCEPT: Graphic Utility
LEVEL: Grades 9 to 12
SOFTWARE TITLE: Colortext
PUBLISHER: Bertamax, Inc.,
                           101 3647 Stoneway N.
                           Seattle, WA 98103
SUGGESTED PRICE: $80.00
HARDWARE: TRS-80
DESCRIPTION: Graphics and text can be used together in Colortext. Colortext provides for high resolution graphics.

CONCEPT: Graphic Utility
LEVEL: Grades 9 to 12
SOFTWARE TITLE: Fontrix 1.1
PUBLISHER: Data Transforms, Inc.,
                           616 Washington St., Suite 106
                           Denver, CO 80203
SUGGESTED PRICE: $75.00
HARDWARE: Apple II+, IIe (48K), DOS 3.3
DESCRIPTION: Fontrix 1.1 is a character generator and a high resolution utility program. Fontrix 1.1 allows the picture to be 16 times larger than the screen. Several pre-designed fonts are provided with the software.
EVALUATION: *Softside*, November, 1983.

CONCEPT: Graphic Utility
LEVEL: Grades 9 to 12
SOFTWARE TITLE: Versawriter
PUBLISHER: Versa Computing, Inc.
                    887 Conestoga Circle
                    Newbury Park, CA 91320
SUGGESTED PRICE: $299.00
HARDWARE: Atari 400, 800 (32K, BASIC cartridge); Apple II Series; IBM
                    PC
DESCRIPTION: Versa Writer allows for the mixing of text and graphics on
                    the same screen. A drawing arm and a plastic tablet allow
                    for tracing and scaling. A shape maker provides the
                    capability to move images around the screen.
EVALUATION: *Softside*, November, 1983.

CONCEPT: Graphic Utility
LEVEL: Grades 9 to 12
SOFTWARE TITLE: Font Master
PUBLISHER: Xetec, Inc.
                    30100 Arnold Rd.
                    Salina, KS 67401
SUGGESTED PRICE: $39.95
HARDWARE: Commodore 64
DESCRIPTION: Font Master allows the user to create signs, posters,
                    banners, etc. using a number of different fonts. Printing
                    can be done in boldface, italics, inverse, or original fonts
                    can be created.
EVALUATION: *Home Computer Magazine*, Vol.5 #5, 1985.

CONCEPT: Graphic Utility
LEVEL: Grades 9 to 12
SOFTWARE TITLE: Graphics Utility
PUBLISHER: Savant Software
                    P.O. Box 440278
                    Houston, TX 72244
SUGGESTED PRICE: $55.00
HARDWARE: IBM PC (64K), Color adaptor
DESCRIPTION: Graphics Utility provides an interactive editor designed to
                    create up to 50 figures or blocks with 39 X 39 pixels. This
                    program is capable of grouping figures to create a complete
                    picture.
EVALUATION: *Softside*, November, 1983.

GRAPHIC UTILITY

CONCEPT: Graphic Utility
LEVEL: Grades 9 to 12
SOFTWARE TITLE: Lumena
PUBLISHER: Time Arts, Inc.
                    3436 Mendecino Ave.
                    Santa Rosa, CA 95401
SUGGESTED PRICE: $495.00
HARDWARE: Mindset, Graphics Tablet
DESCRIPTION: Lumena allows students to design, store and retrieve graphic
                    images. Scaling, rotation and animation are features of
                    Lumena.
EVALUATION: *Creative Computing*, February, 1985.

CONCEPT: Graphic Utility
LEVEL: Grades 9 to 12
SOFTWARE TITLE: Zoom Graphics
PUBLISHER: Phoenix Software
                    64 Lake Zurich Dr.
                    Lake Zurich, IL 60047
SUGGESTED PRICE: $49.95
HARDWARE: Apple II Series (48K)
DESCRIPTION: Zoom Graphics can be used to print small sections of
                    graphic designs as well as full graphic images.
EVALUATION: *InfoWorld*, June 20, 1983.

CONCEPT: Picture and Shapes
LEVEL: Grades K to 7
SOFTWARE TITLE: Facemaker
PUBLISHER: Spinnaker Software, Inc.,
                      One Kendall Square
                      Cambridge, MA   02139
SUGGESTED PRICE: $29.95
HARDWARE: Commodore 64; Apple II
DESCRIPTION: Facemaker allows the user to create cartoon faces and add
                      motion such as: smiling, frowning or winking. Facemaker is
                      menu driven and easy for the young child.
EVALUATION: *Computer and Electronics*, January, 1983.

CONCEPT: Pictures and Shapes
LEVEL: Grades 3 to 6
SOFTWARE TITLE: Picture Play
PUBLISHER: Edu-Pro
                      Knowledge Access, Inc.
                      445 E. Charleston Rd.
                      Palo Alto, CA   94306
SUGGESTED PRICE: $29.95
HARDWARE: Apple II Series, (64K)
DESCRIPTION: Picture Play allows students to develop pictures, patterns
                      and shapes. Further, Picture Play allows students to control
                      music, color, text and pseudo animation.

CONCEPT: Pictures and Shapes
LEVEL: Grades 3 to 7
SOFTWARE TITLE: Little Rembrandt
PUBLISHER: Software Research Corporation
                      3939 Quadra St.
                      Victoria, British Columbia, Canada V8X IJ5
SUGGESTED PRICE: $29.95
HARDWARE: Apple II Series, Joystick
DESCRIPTION: Little Rembrandt allows students to draw, color or erase.
                      Students can draw lines boxes and other shapes to produce
                      pictures.

PICTURES AND SHAPES

CONCEPT: Pictures and Shapes
LEVEL: Grades 3 to 8
SOFTWARE TITLE: Pic Builder
PUBLISHER: Weekly Reader Family Software
                      245 Long Hill Rd.
                      Middletown, CT 06457
SUGGESTED PRICE: $29.95
HARDWARE: Apple II Series; Atari 400, 800, 1200; Commodore 64
DESCRIPTION: Pic Builder provides students with a set of pre-designed
                      images on a disk. Pic Builder also allows students to create
                      their own pictures. This program includes a user's guide, a
                      poster and palette cards for reference.

CONCEPT: Picture and Shapes
LEVEL: Grades 3 to 9
SOFTWARE TITLE: Picturewriter
PUBLISHER: Scarborough Systems, Inc.,
                      25 N. Broadway
                      Tarrytown, NY 10591
SUGGESTED PRICE: $39.95
HARDWARE: Apple II+, IIe
DESCRIPTION: Picturewriter allows the user to create shapes or patterns,
                      paint with color or call up a pre-programmed picture. A
                      tutorial is supplied on the disk.
EVALUATION: *Creative Computing*, February, 1984.

CONCEPT: Pictures and Shapes
LEVEL: Grades 4 to 8
SOFTWARE TITLE: Thorographics
PUBLISHER: Thorobred Software, Inc.
                      10 Olympic Plaza
                      Murray, KS 42071
SUGGESTED PRICE: $59.00
HARDWARE: Apple IIE, Apple II+
DESCRIPTION: With Thorographics, students can draw Hi-Resolution
                      graphics on a screen using the keyboard.

CONCEPT: Pictures and Shapes
LEVEL: Grades 6 to 12
SOFTWARE TITLE: Graphics Magician, Picture Painter
PUBLISHER: Penguin Software
                    P.O. Box 311
                    Geneva, IL 60134
SUGGESTED PRICE: $39.95 - $49.95
HARDWARE: Commodore 64; Atari (48K); IBM PC, PCjr (128K); Apple IIe,
                    IIc (128K, 80 Column)
DESCRIPTION: Graphics Magician, Picture Painter performs the same
                    functions as Graphics Magician with the additional features
                    of 8 brushes and 256 colors. Picture Painter does not have
                    animation capabilities.
EVALUATION: *Popular Computing*, November, 1984.

CONCEPT: Pictures and Shapes
LEVEL: Grades 6 to 12
SOFTWARE TITLE: Shapes
PUBLISHER: Luster Software Services
                    8401 Fountain Ave. #16
                    Los Angeles, CA 90069
SUGGESTED PRICE: $29.95
HARDWARE: Apple II Series
DESCRIPTION: Shapes provides many pre-designed shapes for student use.
                    This program contains character and animation sets as well
                    as flow chart symbols.

CONCEPT: Pictures and Shapes
LEVEL: Grades 6 to 12
SOFTWARE TITLE: Shape Tables
PUBLISHER: MECC
                    3490 Lexington Ave. N.
                    St. Paul, MN 55112
SUGGESTED PRICE: $45.00
HARDWARE: Apple II Series
DESCRIPTION: Shape Tables provides students with several Hi-Resolution
                    graphics shape tables with 187 pre-formed shapes.

PICTURES AND SHAPES

CONCEPT: Pictures and Shapes
LEVEL: Grades 6 to 12
SOFTWARE TITLE: The Graphics Kit
PUBLISHER: Softsync, Inc.
                     14 East 34th St.
                     New York NY 10016
SUGGESTED PRICE: $14.95
HARDWARE: Timex/Sinclair 1000 (16K)
DESCRIPTION: The Graphics Kit allows students to create shapes using
                     characters or geometric shapes through plotting.
EVALUATION: *Micro Computing*, June 1983; *Popular Computing*, March,
                     1984.

CONCEPT: Pictures and Shapes
LEVEL: Grades 6 to 12
SOFTWARE TITLE: Rainbow Graphics
PUBLISHER: Rainbow Computing, Inc.
                     8811 Amigo Ave.
                     Northridge, CA 91324
SUGGESTED PRICE: $29.95
HARDWARE: Apple II Series, Joystick
DESCRIPTION: Rainbow Graphics provides for keyboard design of shapes
                     and picture design with the use of a joystick. Pixel by
                     pixel design functions are available.
EVALUATION: *Popular Computing*, November, 1984.

CONCEPT: Pictures and Shapes
LEVEL: Grades 8 to 12
SOFTWARE TITLE: The Poor Mans Graphics Tablet
PUBLISHER: Rainbow Computing, Inc.
                     8811 Amigo Ave.
                     Northridge, CA 91324
SUGGESTED PRICE: $49.95
HARDWARE: Apple II Series
DESCRIPTION: The Poor Mans Graphics Tablet provides most drawing
                     features found on graphics tablet hardware by only using a
                     keyboard. This program offers brush selection, eight colors
                     and 59 textures as well as text placement.

CONCEPT: Pictures and Shapes
LEVEL: Grades 8 to 12
SOFTWARE TITLE: Super Shape Draw and Animate
PUBLISHER: Avant-Garde, Inc.
                      P.O. Box 30160
                      Eugene, OR 97403
SUGGESTED PRICE: $34.95
HARDWARE: Apple II Series
DESCRIPTION: Super Shape Draw and Animate features diagonal plotting
                      and no-delay viewing of pictures and shapes. This program
                      provides the option to add shapes to the table.

CONCEPT: Picture and Shapes
LEVEL: Grades 9 to 12
SOFTWARE TITLE: PIXIT
PUBLISHER: Baudville Software
                      1001 Medical Park Dr. S.E.
                      Grand Rapids, MI 49506
SUGGESTED PRICE: $49.95
HARDWARE: Apple II Series
DESCRIPTION: PIXIT is a graphics processor which allows for creation of
                      shapes with a shape table. The user can also use
                      pre-designed shapes. A text placement function is also
                      included with this program.
EVALUATION: *Classroom Computer Learning*, November, 1984.

CONCEPT: Pictures and Shapes
LEVEL: Grades 6 to 12
SOFTWARE TITLE: Graphix Artist
PUBLISHER: Sophisticated Software of America
                      198 Ross Rd.
                      King of Prussia, PA 19406
SUGGESTED PRICE: $39.95
HARDWARE: Commodore 64, Joystick; IBM PCjr; MacIntosh
DESCRIPTION: Graphix Artist allows for the creation of detailed color
                      graphic (16 colors) which can be used with other programs.
EVALUATION: *Personal Software*, March, 1984.

PICTURES AND SHAPES

CONCEPT: Picture and Shapes
LEVEL: Grades 9 to 12
SOFTWARE TITLE: Hi-Res Secret
PUBLISHER: Avant - Garde Software
                              P.O. Box 30160
                              Eugene, OR 97403
SUGGESTED PRICE: $129.95
HARDWARE: Apple II Series, Keyboard, Joystick or Paddles
DESCRIPTION: Hi-Resolution Secret is a color palette program that allows the user to fill shapes or pictures and to create and animate shapes. In addition, several colors are available.

CONCEPT: Picture and Shapes
LEVEL: Grades 9 to 12
SOFTWARE TITLE: Screen Artist II
PUBLISHER: The Small System Center
                              P.O. Box 268
                              New Hartford, CT 06057
SUGGESTED PRICE: $29.00
HARDWARE: TRS-80 Model I, III (32K)
DESCRIPTION: Screen Artist II converts images to the BASIC language. Text and graphics can be merged with other BASIC programs.
EVALUATION: *Electronic Learning*, October, 1982.

CONCEPT: Grades 9 to 12
LEVEL: Three Dimensional Graphics
SOFTWARE TITLE: EnerGraphics
PUBLISHER: EnerGraphics Research
                    150 North Meramac, Suite 207
                    St. Louis, MO 63105
SUGGESTED PRICE: $350.00
HARDWARE: IBM PC (128K)
DESCRIPTION: EnerGraphics allows students to create three dimensional
                    images using color, zoom and rotation. In addition, free
                    hand drawing capabilities and perspective features are
                    available with EnerGraphics.
EVALUATION: *PC*, June 17, 1985; *Business Software*, January, 1984.

CONCEPT: Three Dimensional Graphics
LEVEL: Grades 9 to 12
SOFTWARE TITLE: Stereo 3-D Graphics
PUBLISHER: Atari Program Exchange
                    P.O. Box 3705
                    Santa Clara, CA 95055
SUGGESTED PRICE: $24.95
HARDWARE: Atari 400, 800, 1200XL
DESCRIPTION: Stereo 3-D Graphics package allows students to create three
                    dimensional wire drawings. In addition this program allows
                    display of the wire drawings in a see through image format.
                    Images are created by plotting points and connecting points
                    with lines.
EVALUATION: *Popular Computing*, November, 1983.

CONCEPT: Three Dimensional Graphics
LEVEL: Grades 9 to 12
SOFTWARE TITLE: Artwork and Brushwork
PUBLISHER: Westend Film, Inc.
                    2121 Newport Pl. N.W.
                    Washington, DC 20037
SUGGESTED PRICE: $2,450/00 (Artwork), $1,450.00 (Brushwork)
HARDWARE: IBM PC (512K), DOS 2.0
DESCRIPTION: Artwork and Brushwork are high capacity graphics programs
                    which allow for video input. Features include drawing,
                    color shading, three dimensional shape manipulation,
                    animation and illustration of output features.
EVALUATION: *PC*, October 1, 1985.

THREE DIMENSIONAL GRAPHICS

CONCEPT: Three Dimensional Graphics
LEVEL: Grades 9 to 12
SOFTWARE TITLE: 3-D Computer Graphics: Perspective Drawing with the
                    Computer
PUBLISHER: Entelek, Ward Whidden House
                    The Hill, P.O. Box 1303
                    Portsmouth, NH 03801
SUGGESTED PRICE: $75.00
HARDWARE: Apple IIe
DESCRIPTION: With 3-D Computer Graphics, students can generate shapes,
                    learn perspective drawing and manipulate objects in space.
                    Other options include picture construction, advanced
                    projection and three dimensional images.

CONCEPT: Draw and Paint
LEVEL: Grades K to 3
SOFTWARE TITLE: Magic Crayon
PUBLISHER: C and C Software
                    5713 Kentfield Circle
                    Wichita, KS 67220
SUGGESTED PRICE: $35.00
HARDWARE: Apple II Series (48K)
DESCRIPTION: Magic Crayon provides four levels of tutorial learning.
                    Topic levels include draw and design pictures and computer
                    usage. Each level differs in complexity for each topic.
EVALUATION: *InfoWorld*, October 17, 1983.

CONCEPT: Creative Writing and Illustration
LEVEL: Grades 3 to 8
SOFTWARE TITLE: Storymaker
PUBLISHER: Scholastic, Inc.
                    2931 East Mc Carty St.
                    P.O. Box 7502
                    Jefferson City, MO 65102
SUGGESTED PRICE: $39.95
HARDWARE: Apple II Series (64K); Koala Pad, Joystick or Mouse
DESCRIPTION: Storymaker is designed to allow students to combine
                    creative writing and illustration. Students may design their
                    own images or choose pre-designed images to illustrate
                    student generated stories.
EVALUATION: *The Computing Teacher*, February, 1985.

CONCEPT: Creative writing and Illustration
LEVEL: Grades 3 to 9
SOFTWARE TITLE: Bank Street Story Book
PUBLISHER: Mindscape, Inc.
                    3444 Dundee
                    North Brook, IL 60062
SUGGESTED PRICE: $39.95
HARDWARE: Apple II Series (64K); Joystick or Koala Pad
DESCRIPTION: Bank Street Story Maker allows students to combine
                    creative writing and illustration. Students can create a
                    multi-page story with both text and images.
EVALUATION: *The Computing Teacher*, February, 1985.

TUTORIAL

CONCEPT: Draw and Paint
LEVEL: Grades 5 to 12
SOFTWARE TITLE: Paint Magic
PUBLISHER: Data Most, Inc.
                      8943 Fullbright Ave.
                      Chatsworth, CA 91311
SUGGESTED PRICE: $49.95
HARDWARE: Commodore 64 (16K), Joystick
DESCRIPTION: Paint Magic is a draw and paint program that includes such
                      functions as: draw, paint, transpose, grab, slide, merge,
                      restore and shrink. Paint Magic provides a tutorial for self
                      instruction.
EVALUATION: *InfoWorld*, May 21, 1984.

CONCEPT: Perspective
LEVEL: Grades 7 to 12
SOFTWARE TITLE: Art: Perspective Drawing
PUBLISHER: MECC
                      3490 Lexington Ave. North
                      St. Paul, MN 55126
SUGGESTED PRICE: $44.00
HARDWARE: Apple II (48K)
DESCRIPTION: Art: Perspective Drawing is a self-paced tutorial designed to
                      instruct students on one and two point perspective. Printed
                      handouts and a support manual are provided with the
                      software.

CONCEPT: Interior Design
LEVEL: Grades 7 to 12
SOFTWARE TITLE: Floor Plan
PUBLISHER: Charles Clark Co. Inc.
                      168 Express Drive South
                      Brentwood, NY 11717
SUGGESTED PRICE: $39.00
HARDWARE: Apple II Series
DESCRIPTION: Floor Plan allows students to create a room design and
                      experiment with a variety of room arrangements. Templates
                      for furniture are provided to help teach interior design
                      principles. Floor plans are easily manipulated allowing
                      students to experiment.

PART C

EVALUATING SOFTWARE FOR LEARNING OUTCOMES

John B. Cooney

University of Northern Colorado

EVALUATING SOFTWARE FOR LEARNING OUTCOMES

With a growing abundance of educational software, teachers face difficult selection decisions. Often, their choices are made under the constraints of limited funds for computer materials and tight classroom schedules. In these circumstances, teachers seek the educational software most likely to produce **positive learning outcomes**.

Innumerable "software evaluation" systems have emerged to help teachers select software. Unfortunately, nearly all software evaluation systems are heavily weighted on computer-related dimensions such as error-handling, aesthetic considerations, such as the quality of screen displays, and content related issues of scope, sequence, and accuracy. Although important, these characteristics do not address the essential question: **Is the software's design consistent with our knowledge of how students learn?** We contend that an adequate software evaluation model must arise from a clear perspective of the student as a learner.

The text material of this chapter leads to software evaluation questions and a sample software evaluation form. It can serve as a guide to identifying software likely to produce positive learning outcomes. Using this approach does not exclude using additional software evaluation procedures that emphasize computer and curriculum related issues. However, we suggest that if a particular software does not meet our standards of probable learning effectiveness, it is unlikely to prove satisfactory in everyday teaching situations.

HUMAN COGNITION

Over the past decade, research on human cognition has revealed new insights into the mental processes involved in learning, remembering, reasoning, and problem solving. These findings also have implications for the design and evaluation of educational software. An overview of the components, functions and limitations of the human cognitive system provides a framework for understanding why some educational software that "looks good" fails to produce positive learning outcomes.

Noted educational psychologist Robert M. Gagne (1984) identified five categories of learned capabilities involved in complex human performance:

* verbal knowledge
* intellectual skills
* cognitive strategies
* motor skills
* attitudes

These five capabilities are distinguished because each requires its own unique set of **external conditions** such as identifying goals, determining prerequisite knowledge and providing corrective feedback. And acquiring each capability is also contingent on the presence of a unique set of **internal conditions** in a learner: prerequisite verbal knowledge, intellectual skills, motor skills, and attitudes. Therefore, an analysis of the internal and external conditions necessary for acquiring a targeted skill must be part of educational software evaluation.

What are the basic elements of a human cognitive system? Contemporary theory suggests that, at the very least, the model of a human cognitive system must be capable of describing: a) the reception of sensory information; b) how information is represented in memory; c) the different states of information (aware vs. unaware); d) processes related to learning, remembering and thinking; and, e) the generation of overt behavior (Anderson, 1983; Bower, 1975). A model depicting these elements, as they may be affected through the interaction with a computer system, is presented in Figure 1. Arrows in the diagram represent the flow of information from a computer's screen through the various stages of cognitive processing. A careful study of this model and the descriptions of it's components will promote a better understanding of the conditions necessary to achieve a particular learning outcome.

Components of a Sensory System

What is the chain of events involved in a learner's cognitive response to computer produced stimuli? Verbal, auditory, and visual-spatial information from a computer stimulates the learner's sense receptors. In turn, these sense receptors transform the information into neural codes. Neural codes are then preserved, or "stored," briefly, usually a few hundredths of a second, in the learner's short term sensory register (Sperling, 1960). In this brief interval of time, information is preserved virtually exact. However, human attention is limited. Unless a student continuously attends to a computer display, sensory information is quickly lost. Sensory information which does not continue to receive attention "decays," or vacates the sensory register.

It is useful to think of attention as a filter which restricts the amount of information that can make contact with the long-term memory system. Note in Figure 1 that only a few elements of a computer display stored in the sensory register (represented by the arrows) is passed through this attention filter.

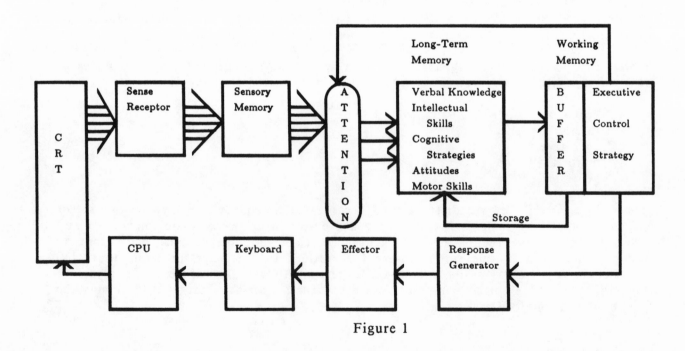

Figure 1

Long-Term Memory

Within a few seconds, sensory information receiving continued attention activates knowledge in long-term memory. Information stored in long-term memory consists of attitudes, beliefs, sequences of motor skills, strategies for learning and problem solving, intellectual skills, and verbal knowledge.

A consistent finding from research on long-term memory for text, pictures, conversations or other events, is that people do not remember exact details. Rather, it appears that our experiences are transformed into an abstract memory code (proposition) that preserves the meaning of an experience. Although controversy remains over exactly how knowledge is stored in long-term memory, current research suggests that it is organized hierarchically. It may be helpful to think about a taxonomy with superordinate and subordinate concepts that are linked together to form a network. Reading a word results in the activation of its long-term memory code and the spreading of activation to related concepts. For example, comprehension of the sentence "mammals are warm-blooded" depends on the activation of information (propositions) related to mammals (e.g., live birth, lungs), specific instances of mammals (e.g., dog, whale, elephant) and being warm-blooded (consistent body temperature). Other knowledge (e.g., intellectual skills, and cognitive strategies) have different representations in long-term memory that will be discussed later in this section.

Working Memory

Verbal knowledge, intellectual skills and cognitive strategies, activated by the information displayed on the computer monitor, become part of the students' working memory system. A useful analogy is to think of working memory as a workbench where conscious mental processing is carried out (Klatzky, 1975). Working memory is a complex and powerful memory system. Note in Figure 1 that working memory consists of a short-term memory buffer capable of holding a small amount of verbal information called "chunks," visual-spatial information and a central executive (Baddeley and Hitch, 1974).

Simon (1980) defines a chunk as any perceptual configuration of visual or auditory stimuli that is familiar and recognizable. Examples of chunks include words, phrases and rules. On the average, the short-term memory buffer can maintain about four chunks of information in an active (conscious) state. However, chunks may be very large and complex. The central executive, governed by the learner's goals and motives, is responsible for selective attention and a variety of other control processes which: a) modify and transform information in the short-term memory buffer; b) store information in long-term memory; and, c) retrieve information from long-term memory.

Storage

First, examine the role of selective attention depicted in Figure 1. Note the arrow that connects the working memory system with the process of attention. Depending on features of the computer display, goals and motives, students will selectively attend to certain information on the display at the expense of other information. Adding (storing) one new chunk of information to long-term memory requires about eight seconds of attention while several minutes of attention may be required to add a complex chunk of information to long-term memory, if the elementary chunks have to be acquired (stored in long-term memory) at the same time (Simon, 1980).

Storage of information in long-term memory can be hastened somewhat by invoking other control processes such as rehearsal, elaboration and organizational strategies. Rehearsal may be thought of as the subvocal recitation of chunks in the short-term memory buffer. Reciting a phone number until it has been dialed, mentally reciting a short list of items needed for the evening meal on the way to the grocery store or the answer to a question asked by a teacher are examples of rehearsal. Interruption of the rehearsal cycle (e.g., a busy signal, a near accident on the way to the store, or a student laughing in the classroom) usually results in the loss of the information from short-term memory. To reactivate information, one must search long-term memory for the phone number, recipe or question. If retrieval failure occurs, we must return to external sources such as the telephone directory, recipe book, or the teacher. Although rehearsal promotes the storage of information in long-term memory, there are more efficient methods.

Adding new chunks of information to long-term memory is facilitated through the control process of elaboration. Elaboration involves the retrieval from long-term memory of additional information that is related to the new chunks of information. Noting similarities and dissimilarities of new information in relation to one's existing knowledge base contributes to the meaning and memorability of new information. Techniques that involve the construction of visual imagery are also considered examples of elaboration strategies. Examples of visual imagery are discussed later in this section. Similarly, organizational strategies consist of a conscious effort to label and categorize the contents of short-term memory. When properly activated, the control processes of rehearsal, elaboration and organization can result in more rapid acquisition and storage of new information as well as more efficient retrieval.

Retrieval

When the short-term memory buffer contains a question proposition, plans for guiding a search of long-term memory are retrieved, or activated, in the working memory system. Retrieval strategies typically involve a systematic plan for selecting cues from questions which are then used to activate relevant knowledge structures in long-term memory. In addition, students use decision rules to determine whether information activated will be useful for answering a question. If a student has used elaboration or organization strategies for storing information, the cues will make quick contact with relevant information. If a question states a problem to be solved, plans for solving the problem are assembled in working memory under the control monitor in much the same way. Each of these processes are described in greater detail in later in this section.

Response Generation and Performance

Plans for achieving a goal are transmitted to a structure called a **response generator**. The response generator selects muscle groups to respond to a goal and preform the necessary sequence of movements. Subsequently, these messages are transmitted to **effectors**, resulting in overt action. In Figure 1, overt actions consist of pressing a key or sequence of keys on a computer's keyboard. Student actions are processed by the instructional program which modifies the information on the monitor and the information processing cycle begins again.

CATEGORIES OF LEARNING OUTCOMES

Verbal Knowledge

Verbal knowledge represents much of what students are expected to learn in school. Verbal knowledge is a fundamental building block for more complex forms of learning. However, the meaning of words is but a small fraction of the verbal knowledge that students are expected to learn. **Discourse** is a complex form of verbal knowledge. Examples of discourse are the pledge of allegiance, national anthem, Bill of Rights, or a poem. Often, students are asked to memorize discourse in verbatim form. However, Gagne warns that verbatim recall of discourse does not guarantee that students have extracted meaning.

People rarely store verbal knowledge verbatim. Verbal knowledge is stored in long-term memory as a collection of **propositions**. A proposition is the smallest unit of knowledge that can stand as a separate assertion (Anderson, 1984). A proposition can be represented as a list consisting of a relational term (verb, adjectives, predicate) and arguments (noun). Relational terms provide connections among the arguments. The general form of a proposition is:

(relation, argument 1, argument 2)

Consider the following statements: "The capital of Colorado is Denver" and "2+3=5". Each statement may be expressed in the following propositional notation:

(is capital of, Denver, Colorado)
(is 5, 2,+3)

Evidence of this underlying structure is provided by the finding that students have difficulty remembering whether they have seen the sentences: "Denver is the capital of Colorado" or "The Capital of Colorado is Denver." Nevertheless they have learned the capital of Colorado. The point is that **memory for verbal information is reconstructive.**

Are propositions stored as a collection of unrelated facts? No, propositions are encoded into long-term memory as organized networks. Depending on instruction and the students' organizational strategies, the associative network of states and capitals may be organized according to geographic region, the alphabet, or order of statehood. Likewise, number facts may be organized by families or in a two dimensional table. Not everyone stores propositions exactly the same.

Working memory extracts propositions from discourse and assembles them to derive meaning from a message. Computer displays containing numerous propositions increase working memory demands and decrease comprehension. Therefore, effective educational software limits the amount of information and propositions presented on a single screen display.

Internal Prerequisites to Verbal Knowledge

Evaluation of software designed to teach verbal knowledge must begin by identifying prerequisite internal conditions of knowledge and skills. Of the two sited propositions above, an evaluator might state that a software's effectiveness depends on students

103

having previously learned concepts of state, capital, numerosity, magnitude, and combination. Also, students must know the linguistic rules underlying comprehension. A learner must possess an equal or higher reading level than required by the computer lesson or frustration will impede acquisition of verbal knowledge.

External Prerequisites to Verbal Knowledge

After identifying necessary internal conditions, an evaluator should identify external prerequisites. First, does the software inform the learner of the lesson's goals and objectives? Second, does the software pretest, activate or teach the internal prerequisites? Other factors having a pronounced effect on verbal knowledge acquisition include:

Selective Repetition with Feedback

Recall and recognition of verbal knowledge improves through repetition. However, students become bored with software that continually repeat well-learned information. Therefore, software that monitors student performance and **presents unlearned items** offers a greater challenge while maximizing learning (Chant & Atkinson, 1978).

Encoding Context

The learning context profoundly affects a students' ability to retrieve information from long-term memory (Bower, 1972; Gartman & Johnson, 1972). Programs presenting verbal information in varied contexts establish more retrieval cues for recalling information.

Organizational Strategies

Teaching strategies for organizing verbal information improves recall by providing a systematic method of searching long-term memory (Bower, Clark, Lesgold, & Winzenz, 1969). Therefore, an evaluator should ask, "Does the software make explicit an organizational strategy for learning and remembering?"

Mnemonic Strategies

Persons demonstrating exceptional memory performance use techniques that make novel information meaningful. One powerful technique, the keyword method, uses imagery to link new information to the learner's existing knowledge base. This technique has been used effectively in learning a second language vocabulary, expanding native language vocabulary, and in learning scientific classification schemes. Even learning disabled students benefit from using mnemonic techniques (Mastropieri, Scruggs, & Levin, 1985).

Evaluation Questions for Verbal Knowledge

* Does the software teach the meaning of concepts as opposed to verbatim learning?

* Does the software assess prerequisite knowledge and skills?

* Does the software teach prerequisite knowledge and skills?

* Does the software link new concepts to existing knowledge?

* Does the software limit the amount of information presented on a single screen?

* Does the software monitor student performance to provide selective repetition and feedback?

* Does the software provide varied contexts for the encoding and retrieval of information?

* Does the software help students tie new information to existing information?

Intellectual Skills

Intellectual skills differ from verbal knowledge. Intellectual skills refer to "knowing how," as opposed to "knowing that" (Gagne, 1985). Intellectual skills, sometimes termed procedural knowledge or production systems, underlay the basic skills of reading, writing, and mathematics. These "basic skills" in turn provide essential procedures for learning about other subjects such as music, social studies or art.

Generally, intellectual skills involve symbol manipulation such as calculating, classifying, distinguishing and transforming symbol systems. Intellectual skills range from simple (calculating a sum of two numbers or forming plurals) to complex (using metaphors and analogies in writing or proving a geometric theorem).

A basic intellectual skill is represented in long-term memory as a production system consisting of rules. Most human behavior is rule governed even if by the wrong rule. This does not mean that an individual can always state the rule used to accomplish a goal. Still, their behavior appears to be rule governed. Young children and many adults cannot state the rules of grammar, yet their language conforms to linguistic rules. For example, when children are asked to form the plural of the nonsense word "wug," a typical reply would be "wugs." This response conforms to the rule: "If the goal is to form a plural noun, and the noun ends in a hard consonant, then generate noun + s."

Intellectual skills are stored in long-term memory as production systems. Production systems are organized as rules consisting of goals, conditions and action propositions. The general form of a production system can be represented as follows:

IF   the goal is to achieve X and condition Y is true
THEN   perform action Z

Consider the production system for achieving subject-verb agreement:

IF   the goal is to achieve subject-verb agreement and the subject is singular
THEN   generate (retrieve) a singular verb

Changes in production systems occur as a child matures and gains experience in symbol manipulation. For example, in learning to perform single digit addition, children use counting strategies. Older children and adults typically retrieve the answer from memory (Ashcraft, 1982). Given the problem 2+3= ?, differences in the production systems of children and adults can be represented as follows:

Child:

> IF   the goal is to find a sum and the two addends are 2 and 3
> THEN   set a counter equal to the largest addend (3) and increment the counter 2 times

Adult:

> IF   the goal is to find a sum and the two addends are 2 and 3
> THEN   search memory to retrieve the answer

Adults typically retain a counting production system and revert to it when memory retrieval fails. Elapsed time in problem solving and the types of errors that children and adults make support this interpretation of simple mental addition.

Acquiring an intellectual skill consists of three stages: cognitive stage, associative stage, and autonomous stage (Anderson, 1983; Fitts & Posner, 1967). Acquiring a skill begins with developing verbal knowledge (cognitive stage) about the steps involved in the skill. That is, students store facts related to a skill in long-term memory by rehearsing the fact while they perform the skill.

When learning to strum a melody's chord progression on a guitar, students must first learn to position their fingers on the fingerboard while striking the strings to produce a chord. Even after students have learned to produce chords in the correct order, in the cognitive stage their knowledge is inadequate for skilled performance. Students must also learn to produce the chords in tempo.

Having established the relevant verbal knowledge in long-term memory, transition to the associative stage begins. With continuing feedback , learners begin to detect and eliminate errors in their understanding of how to perform the skill (play the guitar chords). Associations between components of a skill are strengthened.

Now a learner's knowledge is transformed into a procedural form, a **production system**. Transition to the autonomous stage is characterized by an increase in performance speed and accuracy and the disappearance of verbal mediation during performance. A learner no longer thinks about the required steps. He or she may even lose the ability to articulate the verbal knowledge related to the skill.

Improvements in the performance of an intellectual skill during the autonomous stage occur in smaller and smaller increments. Diminishing returns are associated with practice. There appear to be no cognitive limitations on the speed of performing an intellectual skill during the autonomous stage. Any limitations are imposed by involved musculature or learner motivation.

Internal Prerequisites for Acquiring Intellectual Skills

Evaluating software designed to teach intellectual skills begins with identifying the internal prerequisites for successful learning (e.g., knowledge and skills). An answer to the question, "What verbal knowledge and subordinate skills are learners presumed to possess?", must be obtained.

External Prerequisites to Intellectual Skills

Gagne (1985) provided a concise summary of the external conditions or "events of instruction" necessary for acquiring intellectual skills. An overview of these conditions and their implications for software evaluation follows.

Cognitive Stage

Does instruction begin with a statement of the goals and performance expected when learning is complete? Too often instructional software simply informs learners that they will learn about a subject without stating the conditions or desired outcome. For example, students should be informed that they will learn a two-column procedure for proving two triangles congruent using the side-side-side and side-angle-side postulates. The statement "you will learn geometric proofs" is inadequate.

Does instruction pretest, activate, or teach the components, subordinate verbal knowledge and procedural skills, comprising the intellectual skill? One cannot assume that students possess appropriate internal conditions or that students will recall information on their own.

Associative Stage

Does the software use explicit cues that lead students to associate the components of the skill in the proper order? There should be no mystery shrouding the steps leading to the successful performance of the skill.

Does the instructional software require the learner to demonstrate concrete instances of the rule or procedure? Does the software provide feedback on student understanding of a skill? Ideally, the software should diagnose which skill component is in error. However, here lies a major stumbling block to effective computer-based instruction. Programming computers to provide this kind of feedback has been extremely difficult and found to require tremendous amounts of computing power. The reader is referred to Sleeman and Brown (1982).

Does the software require students to make an explicit verbal statement of the rules underlying a skill? Although a students' ability to state a rule may diminish during the autonomous stage, it is usually helpful for a student to be able to verbalize a rule.

Autonomous Stage

Does the instructional software involve spaced, or distributed, practice? Performance decrements often result from instruction that requires massed,

107

intense practice. For example, spaced practice resulted in superior retention of algebraic rules in contrast to massed practice (Gay, 1973). Another aspect of practice that affects skill acquisition is part vs. whole learning. Does the software attempt to teach the skill in parts or in its entirety. Again, basic research has demonstrated that it is better to teach the entire sequence than subsections of the sequence (Schulz and Gorgein, 1976).

Does the software provide the student with varied contexts to demonstrate the application of the rule? As with verbal knowledge, varied contexts facilitate retrieval and transfer of learning.

Evaluation Questions For Intellectual Skills

* Does the software pretest or teach prerequisite verbal knowledge?

* Does the software describe goals in detail?

* Does the software describe the performance level to be achieved?

* Does the software provide explicit cues to help students correctly sequence component skills?

* Does the software require students to provide concrete examples of a rule or procedure?

* Does the software provide feedback to students, enabling them to check for understanding?

* Can the software diagnose student errors?

* Does the software require students to verbalize their understanding of knowledge or a skill?

* Does the software teach the whole skill as opposed to separate component parts?

* Does the software provide for student practice of the whole skill?

* Does the software provide varied contexts in which students are required to apply a rule?

Cognitive Strategies

Cognitive strategies refer to skills for managing attention, learning, remembering, reasoning and problem solving. They involve knowledge about one's cognitive functions and limitations. In contrast to "knowing that" or "knowing how," cognitive strategies are skills related to "learning how to learn." They support self-instruction and independent learning. In the cognitive model, cognitive strategies are executive control processes carried out in working memory.

Of all learning outcomes, the least is know of processes leading to the acquisition of cognitive strategies and their transfer to novel situations and problems. Nevertheless, the software market is rife with software that claim to develop cognitive strategies.

One example involving the use of computers to teach children problem solving and higher order cognitive strategies is the LOGO language (Papert, 1980). Few educators or computer scientists dispute LOGO's superiority as a programming language. There is skepticism, however, about the claims of learning outcomes resulting from learning how to program in LOGO. Most evidence from well-controlled studies fails to support claims that learning LOGO enhances problem solving skills. When asked to read a LOGO program and describe the function of each line, children could not demonstrate that they understood the concepts of sequentiality, recursion, or conditional statements, despite having used them in their own programs. Furthermore, students who had learned to program in LOGO did not demonstrate better planning skills than students who did not learn to program in LOGO (see Tetenbaum & Mulkeen, 1984 for further discussion).

One purpose for noting LOGO's inadequacies as a means for teaching general problem solving skills is to illustrate the difficulty of teaching general problem solving skills, not to denigrate LOGO. There are many examples of other procedures for directly teaching problem solving that have had little success (Greeno, 1980; Newell, 1980). What has become clear from the research is that problem solving is far too complex to hope for identifying a small set of underlying skills.

Existing data also suggests that problem solving cannot be separated from its content domain. However, before a detailed discussion of the issues and criteria for judging problem solving software, a few of the more cognitive strategies will be addressed. More is known about teaching cognitive strategies related to attention, encoding for storage in long-term memory, and retrieval from long-term memory, than problem solving.

Like any other skill, learning to attend to important aspects of discourse can be taught. A promising technique involves using adjunctive questions inserted in the text (Rothkopf, 1970). Also, teaching students about the structure of text has been found to improve their attention to and their comprehension of important information.

Strategies for encoding, storing, and retrieving information in long-term memory distinguish between "good" and "poor" learners (Rohwer, 1975). Typically, capable learners are aware that if they want to remember a new concept they must do something with the information (Brown, 1978; Flavell, 1976). At the lowest level, this would involve rehearsing the information they wish to retain. However, there are more powerful strategies. Some of these strategies involve elaborating a new concept by relating it to something previously established in memory. Similarly, organizing and categorizing new information is tantamount to developing a plan for retrieving the information later. In other words students learn to use the category label as a retrieval cue. Students may be taught these procedures through the insertion of prompts in the instructional software which require students to engage in a desired type of processing. Again, practice in varied contexts is an instructional component.

A more complex strategy involves using imagery. Information rich in imagery is remembered better than information low in imagery (Paivio, 1971). However, young children have difficulty generating their own imagery for new concepts. An example of this technique is the application of the keyword method for teaching mineral classification, involving hardness (Moh's scale), color, and use. First, students were taught rhyming pegwords for the numbers 1 through 10 to represent the hardness scale (1=bun, 2=shoe, 3=tree, etc.). Then keywords that rhymed with some aspect of the mineral (e.g., pie for pyrite) were taught. For each mineral, an interactive image was developed containing the pegwords (hardness), keywords (rhyming with the mineral), color, and an object describing its use.

For example, the interactive image for pyrite contained a picture of a yellow pie (keyword and color attribute) supported by sticks (pegword for six on the hardness scale) with a bottle of acid (use) being poured onto the pie. This mnemonic technique was superior (94.8% recall) to either a free-study condition (76.7%) where students used their own strategies or a direct instruction procedure (63.5%) where students received drill and practice on recalling the items and their attributes (Mastropieri, Scruggs, McLoone & Levin, 1985). Similar results occurred in foreign language and native language vocabulary acquisition. Finally, learners can be taught to develop their own visual images by demonstrating the technique. With younger children, software shold provide interactive images. For older children and adults, it is better if the software requires the student to generate the interactive image on their own.

Now it is time to revisit issues in teaching problem solving skills. Earlier, the difficulty of separating a problem solving strategy from its content domain (e.g., mathematics) was noted. A detailed description of the problem solving strategies in various content domains would require several chapters if not several volumes. Therefore, only fundamental knowledge about problem solving will be described to derive some general criteria for software evaluation. Readers interested in pursuing this research should consult Mayer (1985) for a discussion of problem solving in mathematics, Chi et al., (1981) for problems solving strategies in physics, and Anderson, Farrell & Saunders (1984), for a comparison of expert and novice problem solving strategies in the development of computer software.

Problem solving behavior is goal directed. The most comprehensive analysis of problem solving was developed by Newell & Simon (1972). In their analysis, problem solving is conceptualized as the process of defining the problem space or state and then searching the problem state for a sequence of actions (operators) that transform the problem from the initial state to the goal state. To illustrate, consider the following algebraic word problem:

> Write an equation to represent the following relationship:
>
> There are twice as many male students on campus as female students. Let M stand for the number of males and F the number of females.

Developing an accurate representation (defining the problem state) of the problem is essential. The stated goal is to write an equation, not solve an equation. If students define the problem state as finding the number of males or females, students will probably decide that the problem cannot be solved and give up. However, if students define the problem state according to the goal provided, searching the problem state for a solution can begin.

Teaching students how to develop an accurate representation of the problem state is among the most difficult and neglected steps in education (Simon, 1980). Many of the errors students make in solving problems involve errors in the translation of a problem into a form that can be solved. For the problem above, it would be common for college students to write the equation as: 2M = F. If students were given the number of females and asked to calculate the number of males they would probably realize that they had made an error in writing the equation. The correct representation is M=2F or 1/2 M=F.

As problems become more complex, people often adopt general strategies in an attempt to find a solution. These general strategies are called heuristics. In contrast to rules or algorithms, which always produce the desired outcome, heuristics do not guarantee a solution. Heuristics are strategies that problem solvers use to guide their search of the problem space. A few of the more well known and successful heuristics are described below (Anderson, 1985; Wickelgren, 1974). Educational software should be carefully examined for these features before any claim is made that the software teaches students to become better problem solvers.

1. Difference-Reduction Method: Does the instructional software require students to set sub-goals that reduce differences between an initial problem state and the goal state?

2. Means-End Analysis: Does the instructional software lead students to: a) create sub-goals by defining the problem state as a collection of differences between the initial state and the goal state, and b) eliminate the most important difference first?

3. Working Backward: Does the instructional software demonstrate how a problem can be decomposed into an hierarchical set of sub-goals, and how solving the sub-goals at the bottom of the hierarchy imply a solution to a problems.

4. Problem Solving by Analogy: Does the instructional software present the solution of a similar problem as a guide to finding the solution of the problem at hand?

5. Contradiction: Does the instructional software emphasize identifying contradictions proving the goal cannot be achieved from the information given?

Although these guidelines for evaluating "problem solving" software are general, they should be useful for determining if the software will be successful in teaching problem solving skills. In using these guidelines, remember that problem solving strategies must be taught in the context of a content domain.

Evaluation Questions for Cognitive Skills

* Does the software pretest for or teach prerequisite verbal knowledge?

* Does the software require students to define a problem?

* Does the software direct students toward a precise goal?

* Does the software require students to set sub-goals?

* Does the software require students to decompose a problem into a hierarchical form and solve from the bottom up?

* Does the software provide a similar problem as a guide?

* Does the instructional software emphasize identifying contradictions?

* Does the software provide a context for the problem?

CONCLUSIONS

Research on cognitive processes underlying human abilities has produced extensive knowledge about learning, remembering, reasoning, and problem solving. Although much remains to be learned the knowledge that has been gained can be put to immediate use in designing and evaluating instructional materials and practices. The purpose of this section has been to provide an overview of cognitive processes and the criteria they imply for evaluating educational software. It is hoped that as a result of this evaluative approach, readers will be able to select better software that will enhance student learning.

REFERENCES

Anderson, J.R. (1983). *The Architecture of Cognition.* Cambridge, MA: Harvard University Press.

Anderson, J.R. (1985). *Cognitive psychology and its implications.* San Francisco, CA: W.H. Freeman.

Anderson, J.R., Farrell, R., and Sauers, R. (1984). Learning to program in LISP. *Cognitive Science, 8,* 87-129.

Atkinson, R.C. and Shiffrin, R.M. (1968). Human memory: A proposed system and its control processes. In K. Spence and J. Spence (Eds.), *The Psychology of Learning and Motivation.* Vol. 2. New York: Academic Press.

Bower, G.H. (1972) Mental imagery and associative learning. In L. Gregg (Ed.), *Cognition in learning and memory.* New York: Wiley.

Bower, G.H. (1975). Cognitive psychology: An Introduction. In W.K. Estes (Ed.), *Handbook of Learning and Cognitive Processes*, Vol. 1. Hillsdale, NJ: Lawrence Erlbaum.

Bower, G.H., Clark, M.C., Lesgold, A.M., and Winzenz, D. (1969). Heirarchical retrieval schemes in recall of categorical word list. *Journal of Verbal Learning and Verbal Behavior, 8,* 323-343.

Brown, A.L. (1978). Knowing when, where, and how to remember: A problem of metacognition. In R. Glasser (Ed.). *Advances in instructional psychology*, Vol. 1. Hillsdale, JN: Lawrence Erlbaum.

Chant, V.G. and Atkinson, R.G. (1978). Application of learning models and optimization theory to problems of instruction. In W.K. Estes (Ed.) *Handbook of Learning and Cognitive Processes*, Vol. 5 Hillsdale, NJ: Lawrence Erlbaum.

Chi, M.T.H., Feltovich, P.J., and Glaser, R. (1981). Categorization and representation of physics problems by experts and novices. *Cognitive Science, 5,* 87-152.

112

Fitts, P.M., and Posner, M.I., (1967) *Human Performance*, Belmont, CA: Brooks Cole.

Flauell, J.J. (1976). Metacognitive aspects of problem solving. In L.B. Resorick (Ed.), *The Nature of Intelligence*. Hillsdale, NJ: Lawrence Erlbaum.

Gay, I.R. (1973). Temporal position of reviews and its effect on the retention of mathematical rules. *Journal of Educational Psychology, 64*, 171-182.

Gagne, R.M. (1985). *The conditions of learning and theory of instruction.* New York: Holt, Rinehart and Winston.

Gartman, L.M., and Johnson, N.F. (1972). Massed versus distributed repetition of homographs: A test of the differential encoding hypothesis. *Journal of Verbal Learning and Verbal Behavior, 11*, 801-808.

Greeno, J.G. (1980). Trends in the theory of knowledge for problem solving. In D.T. Tuman and F. Reif (Eds.), *Problem Solving and Education: Issues in Teaching and Research*. Hillsdale, NJ: Lawrence Erlbaum.

Mastropieri, M.A., Scruggs, T.E. and Levin, J.R. (1985). Mnemonic strategy instruction with learning disabled adolescents. *Journal of Learning Disabilities, 18*, 94-99.

Mayer, R.H. (1985). Mathematical ability. In R.J. Sternberg (Ed.). *Human Abilities: An Information Processing Approach*. SanFrancisco, CA: W.H. Freeman.

Newell, A. (1980). One final word. In D.T. Tuma and F. Reif (Eds.), *Problem Solving and Education: Issues in Teaching and Research*. Hillsdale, NJ: Lawrence Erlbaum.

Newell, A. and Simon, H.A. (1972). *Human Problem Solving*. Englewood Cliffs, NJ: Prentice-Hall.

Paivier, A. (1971). *Imagery and verbal processes*. New York: Holt, Rinehart and Winston.

Papert, S. (1980). *Mindstorms*. New York: Basic Books.

Rohwer, W.D. Jr. (1975). Elaboration and learning in childhood and adolescence. In H.W. Reese (Ed.), *Advances in Child Development and Behavior*. New York: Academic Press.

Rothkopf, E.Z. (1970). The concept of mathemagenic activities. *Review of Educational Research, 40*, 325-336.

Schulz, N. and Gorfein (1976). Subject strategies in part-whole transfer in free recall. *Memory and Cognition, 4*, 311-317.

Simon, H.A. (1980). Problem solving and education. In D.T. Tuma and R. Reif (Eds.), *Problem Solving and Educaiton: Issues in Teaching and Research*. Hillsdale, NJ: Lawrence Erlbaum.

Sleeman, D., and Brown, J.S. (1982). *Intelligent tutoring systems*. New York: Academic Press.

Sperling, G.A. (1980). The information available in brief visual presentation. *Psychological Monographs, 74,* Whole No. 498.

Tetenbaum, T.J. and Hulkeen, T.A. (1984). LOGO and the teaching of problem solving: A call for a moratorium. *Educaitonal Technology, November,* 16-19.

Waugh, N.C. and Norman, D. (1965). Primary memory. *Psychological Review, 72,* 89-104.

Wicklegren, W.A. (1974b). *How to Solve Problems.* New York: W.H. Freeman.

APPENDIX A
SOFTWARE TITLES
INDEX

SOFTWARE LISTING - INDEX

3-D Computer Graphics: Perspective Drawing with the Computer 78, 94
4 - Point Graphics 77
A Child's Imagination 49
Action Art 71
A.G.I.L. Paint Program 67
A2-3D Graphics 53, 84
Alpha Plot 68
Art and Graphics on the Apple II/IIe 64
Art Gallery 69
Art: Perspective Drawing 96
Artist Designer II 75
Artwork and Brushwork 53, 74, 93
Atari Graphics Composer 61
Bank Street Story Book 95
Beagle Graphics 62
Blazing Paddles 66
Color Me: The Computer Coloring Kit 56
Color Paint 59
Color-Craft 50, 63
Colortext 84
Computer Crayons 55
Computer Palette 65
Dazzle Draw 61
Delta Drawing 55
Doodle 59
Dr. Halo 75
Drawing Discovery 56
E-Z Draw 3.3 63
Easel 68
Edu-Paint 62
Electroboard Graphics 66
EnerGraphics 93
ES Painter 64
Facemaker 87
Fingerpaint 57
Floor Plan 96
Flying Colors 71
Font Master 85
FONTRIX 1.1 84
GraForth 52
Graphic Tablet System 76
Graphicmaster 51
Graphics Exhibitor 81
Graphics for the Apple 77
Graphics for the IBM PC 77
Graphics Magician 53
Graphics Magician, Picture Painter 89
Graphics Processing System 74
Graphics Utility 85
Graphiti Is Yours 80

Graphix Artist 91
Graphix Partner 76
Graphx 81
Hi-Res Secret 92
Imigit 74
Joypaint 1.1 69
Koala Painter 58, 79
Little Rembrandt 87
Low and Behold 49, 58
Lumena 73, 86
MacPaint 64
Magic Crayon 55, 95
Magic Paintbrush 61
Mask Parade 79
Micro Painter 57, 70
MousePaint 60
Movie Maker 50
Mr. Pixel's Programming Paint Set 60
Paint 70
Paint Magic 63, 96
Painter Power 62
Paintmaster 73
Paper Graphics 82
Pattern Maker 57
PC Draw 75
PC Paint 67
PC Paint Brush 65
Peripheral Vision 72
Pic Builder 88
Picture Perfect 56
Picture Play 87
Picturewriter 58, 88
PIXIT 91
PM Animator 52
Poster 80
Professor Pixel 49, 66
Rainbow Graphics 90
Rainbow Printer 79
Roger's Easel 60
Screen Artist II 92
Shape Tables 89
SHAPES 89
Sketchpad 71
Sprite Designer 83
Spritemaster 50
Stereo 3-D Graphics 93
Storymaker 95
Super Shape Draw and Animate 91
Super Slide Show 82
Superdraw 67
TAKE 1 52
The Art Studio 80

The Artist 59
The Coloring Book 73
The Complete Graphics System 72
The Digital Paintbrush System 76
The Gibson Light Pen - PenPainter, Mr. Pixel's Cartoon Kit 51
The Gibson Light Pen - PenPainter, PenDesigner, PenAnimator 51, 72
The Graphics Kit 82, 90
The Poor Mans Graphics Tablet 90
The Print Shop 83
The Print Shop Companion, Print Shop GrapThe Print Shop 83
Thorographics 88
U-Draw II 65
Versawriter 85
Video Easel 70
Videogram 68
Videographs 69
VISUALIZER 81
Zoom Graphics 86

APPENDIX B
PUBLISHERS LISTING
INDEX

Academy Software
P. O. Box 9403
San Rafael, CA 94912

Access Software
990 East 900 South
Salt Lake City, UT 84105

Animation Graphics, Inc.
11317 Sunset Hills Rd.
Reston, VA 22090

Apple Computer Co.
10260 Bandley Dr.
Cupertino, CA 95014

Atari Home Computer Division
P. O. Box 61657
Sunnyvale, CA 94086

Atari Program Exchange
P. O. Box 30705
Santa Clara, CA 95055

Avant - Garde Software
P.O. Box 30160
Eugene, OR 97403

Baudville Software
1001 Medical Park Dr. S.E.
Grand Rapids, MI 49506

Beagle Brothers Micro Software
4315 Sierra Vista
San Diego, CA 92103

Bertamax, Inc.,
101 3647 Stoneway N.
Seattle, WA 98103

Brightbill - Roberts, Ltd.
120 E. Washington St. Suite 421
Univ Bldg.
Syracuse, NY 13202

Broderbund Software
17 Paul Dr.
San Rafael, CA 94903

C and C Software
5713 Kentfield Circle
Wichita, KS 67220

Charles Clark Co., Inc.
168 Express Drive South
Brentwood, NY 11717

Chorus Data Systems, Inc.
P.O. Box 370, 6 Continental Blvd.
Merrimack, NH 03054

City Software Distributors, Inc.,
735 W. Wisconsin Ave.
Milwaukee, WI 53233

Classroom Consortia Media, Inc.
57 Bay St.
Staten Island, NY 10301

Comp-Unique
4615 Clausen Ave.
Western Springs, IL 60558

Data Most, Inc.
8943 Fullbright Ave.
Chatsworth, CA 91311

Data Transforms, Inc.,
616 Washington St. Suite 106
Denver, CO 80203

Datasoft, Inc.
19808 Nordhoff Pl.
Chatsworth, CA 91311

Don't Ask Computer Software
2265 Westwood Blvd., Suite B-150
Los Angeles, CA 90064

E&S Software Services
P.O. Box 238
Bedford, MA 01730

Edu-Pro
Knowledge Access, Inc.
445 E. Charleston Rd.
Palo Alto, CA 94306

Edutek Corporation
415 Cambridge #4
Palo Alto, CA 94306

EnerGraphics Research
150 North Meramac Suite 207
St. Louis, MO 63105

Entelek, Ward Whidden House
The Hill, P.O. Box 1303
Portsmouth, NH 03801

Future House
P.O. Box 3470
Chapel Hill, NC 27514

Graphx
P.O. Box C568 Clarence St.
Sydney, NSW Australia 2000

IBM Corporation,
Educational Systems Business Unit
3715 Northside Pkwy
Atlanta, GA 30327

IMSI
633 Fifth Ave.
San Rafael, CA 94901

Individual Software, Inc.
1163 - I Chess Dr.
Foster City, CA 94404

Insoft Corporation
10175 Barbor Blvd. Suite 202B
Portland, OR 97219

Kern International, Inc.
433 Washington St. P.O. Box 1029
Duxbury, MA 02332

Koala Technologies Corporation
3100 Patrick Henry Dr.
Santa Clara, CA 95052

Ksoft
845 Wellner Rd.
Naperville, IL 60540

Luster Software Services
8401 Fountain Ave. #16
Los Angeles, CA 90069

Maximus, Inc.
6723 Whitter Ave.
McLean, VA 22101

MECC
3490 Lexington Ave. N.
St. Paul, MN 55112

Media Cybernetics
7042 Carroll Ave.
Takoma Park, MD 20912

Methods and Solutions, Inc.
300 Unicorn Park Dr.
Woburn, MA 01801

Micro Grafx
1701 North Greenville Ave. Suite
703
Richardson, TX 75081

Micro Lab
2699 Skokie Valley Rd.
Highland Park, IL 60035

Micro Power and Light Co.
12820 Hillcrest Rd. #224
Dallas, TX 75230

Mindscape, Inc.
3444 Dundee Rd.
Northbrook, IL 60062

Monument Computer Service
P.O. Box 603
Joshua Tree, CA 92252

Mouse Systems
23364 Walsh Ave.
Santa Clara, CA 95051

Muse Software
347 N. Charles St.
Baltimore, MD 21201

Nova Software
P.O. Box 545
Alexandria, MN 56308

Pcomputer Pictures
53 Sherman Ave.
Rockville Center, NY 11570

Penguin Software
P.O. Box 311
Geneva, IL 60134

Phoenix Software
64 Lake Zurich Dr.
Lake Zurich, IL 60047

Radio Shack
1800 One Tandy Center
Fort Worth, TX 76102

Rainbow Computing, Inc.
8811 Amigo Ave.
Northridge, CA 91324

Reston Publishing Co.
11480 Sunset Hills Rd.
Reston, VA 22090

San Juan School District
614 Sutter Ave.
Carmichael, CA 95608

Savant Software
P.O. Box 440278
Houston, TX 72244

Scarborough Systems, Inc.
25 N. Broadway
Tarrytown, NY 10591

Scholastic, Inc.
2931 East Mc Carty St.
P.O. Box 7502
Jefferson City, MO 65102

Sim Computer Products
P.O. Box 7
Miquon, PA 19452

Sirius Software
10398 Rockingham Dr. #12
Sacramento, CA 95827

Softel, Inc.,
34 1/2 St. Mark's Place
New York, NY 10003

Softsync, Inc.
14 East 34th St.
New York NY 10016

Software Research Corporation
3939 Quadra St.
Victoria, British Columbia, Canada
V8X IJ5

Software Tech For Computers
P.O. Box 428
Belmont, MA 02178

Sophisticated Software of America
198 Ross Rd.
King of Prussia, PA 19406

Southwestern Data Systems
P.O. Box 582
Santee, CA 92071

Spectrum Holobyte, Inc.
1050 Walnut St. Suite 525
Boulder, CO 80302

Spinnaker Software, Inc.
One Kendall Square
Cambridge, MA 02139

Springboard Software
Charles Clark Co., Inc.
168 Express Dr. South
Brentwood, NY 11717

Stoneware, Inc.
50 Belvedere St.
San Rafael, CA 94901

Sublogic Corporation
713 Edgebrook Dr.
Champaign, IL 61820

Texas Instruments, Inc.,
P.O. Box 53
Lubbock, TX 79408

The Computer Colorworks/Jandel
Scientific
3030 Bridgeway
Saulsalito, CA 94965

The Small System Center
P.O. Box 268
New Hartford, CN 06057

Thorobred Software, Inc.
10 Olympic Plaza
Murray, KS 42071

Tid Bit Software
P.O. Box 5579
Santa Barbara, CA 93018

Time Arts, Inc.
3436 Mendecino Ave.
Santa Rosa, CA 95401

Trillium Press
P.O. Box 921
Madison Square Station
New York, NY 10159

Versa Computing, Inc.
887 Conestoga Circle
Newbury Park, CA 91320

Versa Computing
3541 Old Conejo Rd. Suite 104
Newbury Park, CA 91320

Weekly Reader Family Software
245 Long Hill Rd.
Middletown, CT 06457

Westend Film, Inc.
2121 Newport Pl. N.W.
Washington, D.C. 20037

Wiley Professional Software
605 Third Ave.
New York, NY 10158

Xetec, Inc.
30100 Arnold Rd.
Salina, KS 67401

Z - Soft, International
Microcomputer Software
633 5th Ave.
San Rafael, CA 94901

APPENDIX C
SAMPLE SOFTWARE EVALUATION FORM

A Sample Software Evaluation Form

The following is a **sample software evaluation form** based on principles outlined in EVALUATING SOFTWARE FOR LEARNING OUTCOMES. No single evaluation form is best for every application. Use this software evaluation form only as a guide. Emphasize the questions that are most applicable to your teaching situation. Not all questions will apply to all teaching situations. Place less emphasis on what is less important in your classroom.

Software Title:

Publisher:

Price:

Required Hardware:

Description:

Verbal Knowledge

List the types of verbal knowledge that are intended to be taught by this software:

a)	f)
b)	g)
c)	h)
d)	i)
e)	j)

1=Strongly Disagree 2=Disagree 3=Agree 4=Strongly Agree

1 2 3 4   The software teaches the meaning of
              concepts as opposed to verbatim learning.

1 2 3 4   The software assesses prerequisite knowledge
              and skills.

1 2 3 4   The software teaches prerequisite knowledge
              and skills.

1 2 3 4   The software links new concepts to existing
              knowledge.

1 2 3 4   The software limits the amount of
              information presented on a single screen.

1 2 3 4   The software monitors student performance
              to provide selective repetition and feedback.

1 2 3 4   The software provides varied contexts for
the encoding and retrieval of information.

Intellectual Skills

List the types of intellectual skills that are intended to be taught by this
software:

a)   f)

b)   g)

c)   h)

d)   i)

e)   j)

1=Strongly Disagree 2=Disagree 3=Agree 4=Strongly Agree

1 2 3 4   The software pretests or teaches prerequisite
verbal knowledge.

1 2 3 4   The software describes goals in detail.

1 2 3 4   The software describes the performance level
to be achieved.

1 2 3 4   The software provides explicit cues to help
students correctly sequence component skills.

1 2 3 4   The software requires students to provide
concrete examples of a rule or procedure.

1 2 3 4   The software provides feedback to students,
enabling them to check for understanding.

1 2 3 4   The software diagnoses student errors.

1 2 3 4   The software requires students to verbalize
their understanding of knowledge or a skill.

1 2 3 4   The software teaches the whole concept or
skill as opposed to separate component parts.

1 2 3 4   The software provides for student practice
of the whole concept or skill.

1 2 3 4   The software provides varied contexts in
which students are required to apply a rule.

Cognitive Strategies

List the types of cognitive strategies that are intended to be taught by this software:

a)   f)
b)   g)
c)   h)
d)   i)
e)   j)

1=Strongly Disagree 2=Disagree 3=Agree 4=Strongly Agree

1 2 3 4   The software pretests or teaches prerequisite verbal knowledge.

1 2 3 4   The software requires students to define a problem.

1 2 3 4   The software directs students toward a precise goal.

1 2 3 4   The software requires students to set sub-goals.

1 2 3 4   The software requires students to decompose a problem into a hierarchical form and solve from the bottom up.

1 2 3 4   The software provides a similar problem as a guide.

1 2 3 4   The instructional software emphasizes identifying contradictions.

1 2 3 4   The software provides a context for the problem.

M.